THE
SACRED
PATH TO
Contentment

THE
SACRED
PATH TO
Contentment

Meditations for the

Nurture and Discipline

of the Inner Life

Kenneth H. Stephens
EDITOR

BROADMAN
&HOLMAN
PUBLISHERS

Nashville, Tennessee

0-8054-0199-7

Published by Broadman & Holman Publishers, Nashville, Tennessee
Acquisitions and Development Editor: William D. Watkins
Typesetter: Leslie Joslin

Dewey Decimal Classification: 248.4
Subject Heading: SPIRITUAL LIFE—CHRISTIANITY
Library of Congress Card Catalog Number: 97-46377

Paillettes d'Or originally compiled by Adrien Sylvain. Translated
and abridged from the French by E. L. E. B. Revised and updated for
the modern reader by K. H. Stephens.

Library of Congress Cataloging-in-Publication Data

Stephens, K. H. (Kenneth H.), 1951–
    [Paillettes d'or. English]
    The sacred path to contentment : meditations for the nur-
ture and discipline of the inner life / K. H. Stephens.
        p. cm.
    ISBN 0-8054-0199-7
    1. Spiritual life—Christianity—Quotations, maxims, etc.
I. Title.
BV4513.S7413   1998
248.4—dc21   97-46377
                                        CIP

1 2 3 4 5   02 01 00 99 98

For those who have gradually withdrawn
from a relationship with God,
and losing peace within, weep,
yet dare not return.
May you find hope and peace

CONTENTS

* * * * *

PREFACE

❖ ❖ ❖ ❖ ❖

In the insightful preface to his classic book, *The Knowl-edge of the Holy*, A. W. Tozer observes of modern Christians,

> We have lost our spirit of worship and our ability to withdraw inwardly to meet God in adoring silence. Modern Christianity is simply not producing the kind of Christian who can appreciate or experience the life in the Spirit. The words, "Be still, and know that I am God," mean next to nothing to the self-confident, bustling wor-shiper in this middle period of the twentieth century.
>
> This loss of the concept of majesty has come just as the forces of religion are making dramatic gains and the churches are more prosperous than at any time within the past several hundred years. But the alarming thing is that our gains are mostly external and our losses are

* * * * *

wholly internal; and since it is the quality of our religion that is affected by internal conditions, it may be that our supposed gains are but losses spread over a wider field. [*]

As you read this book, you will catch a fresh glimpse of the spiritual life. In these pages you will find that it is a life of contentment. The strengthening of it has a softening influence, and it is a labor that never wearies, never deceives, but each day is fresh cause for joy. It is called the inner life, and it is our purpose to point out its nature, excellence, means, and hindrances. The inner life is an abiding sense of God's presence. Come and travel the sacred pathway to contentment. See that it is truly good.

---

* A. W. Tozer, *The Knowledge of the Holy* (New York: Harper Collins, 1961), viii.

ACKNOWLEDGMENTS

◆ ◆ ◆ ◆ ◆

Thanks to Gary Heskje, who recognized the value of this collection of writings, and to my daughter, Cindy Blades, who assisted in the preparation of the manuscript. Profound gratitude to the anonymous saints, now in heaven, who preserved for us in writing, these golden counsels.

INTRODUCTION

* * * * *

In the south of France, during the summer, little children and the old and infirm poor, though incapable of hard work, must earn a livelihood, so they employ themselves in searching the beds of dried-up rivers. They search for "Paillettes d'Or," or golden dust, that sparkles in the sun and is carried away by the flowing water. What is done by these poor people and little children for the gold dust God has sown in those obscure rivers, we should do with the counsels and teachings that God has sown almost everywhere. Counsels that sparkle, enlighten, and inspire for a moment, then disappear, leaving only regret that the thought was not collected and treasured.

Who is there that has not experienced at some time in his life those teachings so soft and gentle, yet so forcible, that they make the heart thrill, and reveal to it suddenly a world of peace, joy, and devotion?

It may have been but a word read in a book or a sentence overheard in conversation that may have had for us a double meaning and, in passing, left us touched with an unknown power.

It was the smile on the lips of a loved one whom we knew to be sorrowful that spoke to us of the sweet joy of resignation.

It was the transparent look of an innocent child that revealed to us all the beauty of frankness and simplicity.

Oh, if we had but treasured all the rays of light that cross our path and sparkle only for a moment. Oh, if we had engraved them on our hearts. What a guide and comfort they would have been to us in the days of discouragement and sorrow! What wonderful counsels to guide our actions! What consolations to soothe the broken heart!

How many new ways of doing good!

It is this simple work of gathering a little from every source—from nature, from books, and above all, from life itself. That is the intention of one of your fellow creatures, dear soul, for you who long so to make your life more holy and devout!

And as the gold dust, just gathered and accumulated from the river's bed, was the means of bringing a little profit to the poor person's table and hearth, so would I endeavor to carry a little joy to your heart and peace to your soul.

Gather then these little counsels. Gather them with watchfulness. Let them for a moment penetrate deep into your heart. Then scatter them abroad again that they may go with their good words to the help of others.

They will not come at an inopportune time—will not even ask to be preserved. They do not desire fame. All that they seek is to convey a brief blessing.

PART ONE
The Secret of Contentment

I

"My Lord!" exclaimed a devout soul, "Give me every day a little work to occupy my mind. A little suffering to sanctify my spirit. A little good to do to comfort my heart."

II

If by our deeds we demonstrate our sainthood, then also by our deeds shall we be judged.

Yes, it is little by little that we press onward either toward salvation or eternal ruin. And when at last we reach the gate

* * * * *

of glory or that of punishment, the cry escapes our lips, "The time has come already!"

The first backward step is almost imperceptible; it was those tiny flakes of snow, seeming to melt as they touched the earth, but falling one upon another, that have formed that immense mass that seems ready to fall and crush us.

Ah, if I tried to trace back to what first led to that wrong act—the thought that produced the desire, the circumstance that gave rise to the thought—I should find something almost imperceptible. Perhaps a word with a double meaning I had heard and at which I had smiled; a useless explanation, sought out of mere curiosity; a hasty look, cast I knew not where, and that conscience prompted me to check; a prayer neglected because it wearied me; or work left undone, while I indulged in some daydream, that flitted before my fancy. . . .

A week later, the same things occur, but this time more prolonged, and the stifled voice of conscience is hushed.

Yet, another week. . . . Alas, let us stop there. Each can complete the sad story for himself since it is easy to draw the practical conclusion.

III

A young girl, in one of those moments when the heart seems to overflow with devotion, wrote thus in her journal: "If I dared, I would ask God why I am placed in the world. What have I to do? I do not know. My days are idly spent, and I do not even regret them. If I might but do some good to myself or another, if only for the short space of a minute in each day!" A few days later, when in a calmer mood she reread these lines, she added, "Why, nothing is easier! I have but to give a cup of cold water to one of Christ's little ones."

Yes, even so small a gift as that, but given in God's name, may be of service and gives you the right to hope for a reward in heaven.

Even less than that: a word of advice, something lent to another, a little annoyance patiently borne, a prayer for a friend offered to God, the fault or thoughtlessness of another forgiven without his knowledge—God will repay it all a thousand times!

IV

Gifts given in secret. That is the charity that brings a blessing.

What sweet enjoyment to be able to shed a little happiness around us!

What an easy and agreeable task is that, of trying to make others happy.

Father, if I try to please and imitate you, will you indeed bless me? Thanks! Thanks be to you.

V

Is it fair always to forget all the good or kindness shown to us by those with whom we live, for the sake of one little pain they may have caused us that, most likely, was quite unintentional on their part?

VI

When you sometimes find in books advice or examples that you think may be of service, you take care to copy and consult it as divine revelation. Do as much for the good of your soul. Engrave in your memory, and even write down, the counsels and precepts that you hear or read. Then, from time to time, study this little collection, which you will prize no less than if you had made it all yourself.

Books written by others become tiresome to us in time. But of those we write ourselves we never tire. And it will be yours, this collection of thoughts chosen because you liked them: counsels you have given yourself and moral principles you have discovered that, perhaps, you have proven to be true.

Happy is the soul that each day reaps its harvest.

VII

Do you wish to live at peace with all the world? Then practice the maxims of an influential man who when asked, after the Revolution, how he managed to escape the executioner's ax replied, "I made myself of no reputation and kept silence."

Would you live peaceably with the members of your family, above all with those who exercise a certain control over you? Use the means employed by a pious woman who had to live with someone of a trying disposition:

"I do everything to please her."

"I fulfill all my duties with a smile, never revealing the trouble it causes me."

"I bear patiently everything that displeases me."

❖   ❖   ❖   ❖   ❖

"I consult her on many subjects of which, perhaps, I may be the better judge."

Would you be at peace with your conscience? Let the Spirit of God find you at each moment of the day doing one of these four things that once formed the rule of a saintly life: (1.) praying, (2.) working, (3.) striving after holiness, (4.) practicing patience.

Would you become holy? Try to add to the above actions the following virtues: discipline, faith, spiritual combat, and perseverance.

Finally, if you would live in an atmosphere of benevolence, make it your practice to always be rendering service to others and never hesitate to ask the same of them.

In offering help, you make a step toward gaining a friend. In asking for help, you please others by demonstrating your confidence in them. The result will be a constant habit of mutual patience and a willingness to help in matters of greater importance.

VIII

When teaching or working with others, never laugh or make fun of their awkwardness. If it is caused by stupidity, your laughter is uncharitable. If from ignorance, your mockery is, to say the least, unjust.

Teach the unskilled with gentleness. Show them the right way to work, and God, who sees all your efforts, will smile on your patience and send you help in all your difficulties.

IX

When the heart is heavy and we suffer from depression or disappointment, how thankful we should be that we still have work and prayer left to comfort us. Work forcibly diverts the mind and prayer sweetly soothes the soul.

"Then," writes one who had been sorely tried, "I tell my griefs to God, as a child tells his troubles to his mother. When I have told all, I am comforted, and repeat with a lightened heart, the prayer of St. Francis de Chantal (who certainly suffered more than I.) 'Thy will be done for ever and ever, O Lord, without *If* or *But,*' . . . and then for fear a murmur may arise in my heart, I return immediately to my work and become absorbed in occupation."

X

He who is never satisfied with anything, satisfies no one.

XI

Are there many who try to be of some little help or comfort to the souls with whom they are brought in contact
through life?

Poor souls that perhaps have no longer strength nor will
to manifest the longing they experience, and who lose strength
for want of help without being aware that they are perishing.
Oh, mingle sometimes with your earthly help the blessed
name of God. If there remain one little spark of life in the
soul, that name will rekindle it and carry comfort and peace,
even as air breathed into the mouth of anyone apparently dead
rushes into the lungs and revives the one who is suffering, if
but one breath of life remains.

Souls! Souls! I long for souls!

This is the cry of the Savior. For their sakes he died on
the cross and remains until eternity their Intercessor.

Souls! Souls! I must win souls!

It is the cry of Satan. To obtain them he scatters gold to
tempt them, multiplies their pleasures and vanities, and gives
the praise that only causes vanity and pride.

Souls! Souls! We long for souls!

Let this be our aim, readers and writers of these our "Paillettes"; and for the sake of even one soul, let not fatigue, expense, or the criticism of the world deter us. . . .

XII

How few there are who would dare to address God this way each night: "Lord, deal with me tomorrow as I have this day dealt with others, such as those to whom I was harsh, and because of malice or to show my own superiority I exposed their failings. Others, to whom because of pride or dislike I refused to speak—one I have avoided and another I cannot like because she displeases me—and I will not forgive, nor will I show any kindness toward them."

And yet, let us never forget that sooner or later God will do to us even as we have done to them.

XIII

"Grant me, O Lord," said a humble soul, "that I may pass unnoticed through the world."

This should be the desire, or rather the goal, of all true devotion.

Small virtues require the praise of man to sustain them just as little children require encouragement to walk or stand alone.

But true virtue goes quietly through the world, scattering good around and performing noble deeds without even the knowledge that what it does is heroic.

XIV

One day St. Chantal was excusing herself to St. Francis de Sales for having spoken hastily to someone on the plea that it was in the cause of justice. The Saint replied, "You have been more just than righteous, but we should be more righteous than just."

XV

A devout woman once wrote thus: "In my own family, I try to be as little in the way as possible, satisfied with everything, and never believe for a moment that anyone means unkindness toward me.

"If people are friendly and kind to me, I enjoy it. If they neglect me or leave me, I am always happy alone. It all contributes to my one aim: forgetfulness of self in order to please God."

XVI

Learning is not without its effect on the soul. It either lends the soul wings to bear it up to God or leaves behind its tiny sparks, which little by little consume the whole being.

If you would ascertain all the good or ill you have derived from all those hours devoted to historians, poets, novelists, or philosophers, put to yourself these questions: Since acquiring this knowledge, am I wiser? Am I better? Am I happier?

Wiser. More self-controlled, less the slave of my passions, less irritated by small annoyances, stronger in bearing misfortunes, more careful to live for eternity.

Better. More patient toward others, more forgiving, less unloving, more reluctant to expose the faults of others, more concern for the happiness of those around me.

Happier. More contented with my station in life, striving to derive all possible benefits from it to beautify rather than to alter it.

Have I more faith in God and more calmness and peace in all the events of life?

If you cannot reply in the affirmative, then examine your heart thoroughly, and you will find there, stifling the good that God has implanted, these three tyrants that have obtained dominion over you: pride, ambition, and self-conceit.

* * * * *

From them have sprung dissatisfaction and contempt of your life and its surroundings, restlessness, a longing for power and dominion over others, malice, habitual discontent, and constant complaining. Have you any further doubts? Then inquire of those with whom you live.

Ah, if this be indeed the sad result then, whatever may be your age, close, oh close those books and seek once more those two elements of happiness you never should have forsaken and that, had you made them the companions of your study, would have kept you pure and good.

I refer to prayer and physical labor.

XVII

Listen to the story of a simple shepherd, given in his own words: "I forget now who it was that once said to me, 'Jean Baptiste, you are very poor?' True. 'If you fell ill, your wife and children would be destitute?' True. And then I felt anxious and uneasy for the rest of the day.

"In the evening, wiser thoughts came to me, and I said to myself, 'Jean Baptiste, for more than thirty years you have lived in the world. You have never possessed anything, yet still you live on and have been provided each day with nourishment, each night with rest. Of trouble, God has never sent

❖   ❖   ❖   ❖   ❖

you more than your share. Of help, the means have never failed you. To whom do you owe all this? To God. Jean Baptiste, be no longer ungrateful and banish those anxious thoughts. What could ever induce you to think that the hand from which you have already received so much would close against you when you grow old and have greater need of help?' I finished my prayer and felt at peace."

XVIII

The work of the Sower is given to each of us in this world, and we fall short of our duty when we let those with whom we come into contact leave us without having been given a kind thought. Nothing is so sad as the cry, "I am useless!" Happily none need ever be so.

A kind word, a gentle act, and a loving smile are as so many seeds that we can scatter every moment of our lives that will always spring up and bear fruit.

Happy are those who have many people around them. They are rich in opportunities and may sow bountifully.

XIX

No position in life is so full of opportunities as that of the mother of a family or lady of a house. She may have a dozen interruptions while writing one letter or paying one bill. What holiness, what self–control is needed to be always calm and unruffled amid these little aggravations, and never to manifest the slightest impatience!

Leaving the work without apparent annoyance, replying with a smile on the lips, awaiting patiently the end of a long conversation, and finally returning calmly to the yet unfin–ished work. All this is the sign of a contented soul—of one who waits on God.

Oh, what blessings are shed around them by such patient souls, but, to our sorrow, how rarely we meet with them!

XX

There are times in life when all the world seems to turn against us. Our motives are misunderstood, our words twisted, a malicious smile or an unkind word reveals to us the unfriendly feelings of others, or our advances are repulsed or met with icy coldness.

Oh, how hard it all seems, especially when we cannot discover the cause.

Courage and patience, poor sad one. God is making a furrow in your heart where he will surely sow his grace.

It is rare when injustice or offenses patiently born do not leave the heart filled with marvelous joy and peace at the close of the day.

It is the seed God has sown springing up and bearing fruit.

XXI

That which costs little is of little worth. This thought should make us tremble. In our self-examination we may experience a certain satisfaction at times in noticing the little virtues we may possess and, above all, those that render us pleasing in the eyes of others.

For instance, we may like to pray at a certain place with certain feelings. We think ourselves devout. We are gentle, polite, and smiling toward one person in particular. We are patient with those we respect or in whose good opinion we would like to stand. We are devoted, loving, and generous because the heart experiences an unspeakable pleasure in spending and being spent for others. We suffer willingly at the hands of someone we love and then say we are patient. We are silent because we have no inclination to speak. We avoid society because we fail to shine there, and then act as if we love solitude.

Take these virtues that give you such self-satisfaction and ask yourself at what sacrifice, labor, cost, or care, above all, you have managed to acquire them. Alas, you will find that all that patience, generosity, and piety are but as nothing, springing from a heart puffed up with pride. It costs nothing and it is worthless.

As self-sacrifice, says De Maistre, is the basis and essence of virtue, so those virtues are the most valuable that have cost the greatest effort to attain.

Do not look with so much pride on this collection of virtues, but rather bring yourself to account for your faults. Take just one, the first that comes—impatience, laziness, gossip, an unloving attitude, pouting, whatever it may be—and attack it bravely.

It will take at least a month, counting on three victories every day, not to eradicate it (a fault is not so short lived), but to prevent its attaining dominion over you.

That one subdued, then take another. It is the work of a lifetime. Truly, to our faults may we apply the saying, "Quand il n'y en a plus, il y en a encore."

"Happy should I think myself," said St. Francis de Sales, "if I could rid myself of my imperfections but one quarter of an hour previous to my death."

XXII

Before Worship

JESUS

My child, it is not wisdom I require of you. It is enough if you love me well.

Speak to me as you would talk to your mother if she were here pressing you to her heart.

❖   ❖   ❖

Have you none for whom you would intercede? Tell me the names of your relatives and your friends. At the mention of each name, add what you would have me do for them. Ask much fervently. The generous hearts that forget themselves for others are very dear to me.

Tell me of the poor you would help, the sick you have seen suffering, the sinful you would reclaim, and the estranged you would receive to your heart again.

Pray fervently for all humankind.

Remind me of my promise to hear all prayers that proceed from the heart. The prayer offered for one who loves and is dear to me is sure to be heartfelt and fervent.

* * * * *

* * *

Have you no favors to ask of me? Give me, if you will, a list of all your desires, all the wants of your soul. Tell me, simply, of all your pride, sensuality, self-love, and laziness. Ask for my help in thy struggles to overcome them.

Poor child, do not be ashamed. Many that had the same faults to contend against are now saints in heaven.

They cried to me for help and by degrees they conquered.

Do not hesitate to ask for temporal blessings, health, intellect, or success. I can bestow it and never fail to do so, where it tends to make the soul more holy. What would you desire this day, my child? . . . If you only knew how I long to bless you!

* * *

Have you no interests that occupy your mind?

Tell me of them all . . . of your job. What do you think? What do you desire? Would you give pleasure to your mother, your family, and those in authority over you? What would you do for them?

And for me, have you no passion? Do you not desire to do some good to the souls of those you love, but who are forgetful of me?

* * * * *

Tell me of one in whom you have interest . . . the motive that spurs action . . . the means you would employ.

Lay before me your failures, and I will teach you the cause.

Who would you have to help you? The hearts of all are in my keeping, and I lead them gently, wherever I will. Rest assured: all who need you, I will place around you.

Oh! My child, tell me of all your weariness. Who has grieved you? Who has treated you with contempt and wounded your pride?

Tell me all, and you will end by saying all is forgiven, all forgotten . . . and I, surely I will bless you!

Are you fearful of the future? Is there in your heart that vague dread that you cannot define, but that still torments you?

Trust in my providence . . . I am present with you, I know all, and I will never leave you nor forsake you.

Are there around you those who seem less devout than before, whose coldness or indifference has estranged you from them without real cause?

Pray for them. I can draw them back to you if they are necessary to the sanctification of your soul.

What are the joys of which you would like to tell me?

Let me share your pleasure. Tell me of all that has occurred since yesterday to comfort you, please you, and give you joy!

That fear suddenly dispelled, that unexpected success, that token of affection or the trial that proved you stronger than you thought. . . . My child, I sent it all. Why not show some gratitude and simply thank your Lord?

Gratitude draws down a blessing, and the Great Benefactor likes his children to remind him of his goodness.

Have you no promises to make me?

I can read your heart. You know it. You may deceive man, but you can never deceive God. Be sincere.

Are you resolved to avoid all occasions of wrongdoing? To renounce that which tempts you and never again to open the book that wrongly excites your imagination? Not to give your affection to one who is not devoted to God and whose presence steals the peace from your soul?

Will you go now and be loving and patient toward one who has offended you?

Good, my child. Go, then, and return to your daily toil. Be silent, humble, patient, and charitable. Then return to me with a heart yet more loving and devoted, and I shall have for you fresh blessings.

XXIII

"There will soon be none left," said St. Francis de Sales, "who will love poor sinners, but God and myself."

Oh, why do we fail in love toward those poor sinful ones! Are they not very much to be pitied?

When they are prosperous, pray for them. But when misfortune comes (and trouble weighs heavily on the wicked)—death depriving them of the only beings they did not hate, afflicting them with a loathsome disease, or delivering them up to scorn and misery—oh, then when all this comes upon them, love them freely. It is by affection alone that we can reach the worst characters and the souls that are steeped in sin!

How many have died without repenting who, if only someone had cared for them and shown them love, might have become saints in heaven. Oh, the sins that are committed. Oh, the souls we allow to wander from God and all because we are so lacking in love toward them.

XXIV

Let us always be on our guard against prejudice.

Some people have a way (of which they themselves are unconscious) of turning the cold shoulder to some member of their family.

* * * * *

For what reason? They cannot say because the reason is never very clearly defined, and in this lies all the trouble.

Perhaps an air of indifference they may have imagined and that arose merely from fatigue, or a problem that could not be confided to them. . . .

A word misinterpreted because heard at a time when they felt discontented, and their morbid imagination made every-thing appear in a false light. . . .

Some scandal, to which they ought never to have listened, or at least, should have tried to understand by going directly to the person concerned and seeking an explanation. . . .

And, behold the result: they in their turn become cold, reserved, and suspicious—misinterpreting the slightest gesture. . . . In a few days arises a coldness from the feeling they are no longer loved. Then follow contempt and mistrust. Finally, a hatred that gnaws and tears the very heart.

It all springs up quite unnoticed, until at last the family life is one of bitterness and misery.

They console, or better still, excuse themselves with the thought of their suffering, never considering how much pain they give to others nor where the fault lies.

XXV

Let it rest! Ah, how many hearts on the brink of anxiety and unrest have been made calm and happy by this simple sentence!

Some event has wounded us by its lack of tact. Let it rest; no one will think of it again.

A harsh or unjust sentence irritates us. Let it rest. Whoever may have expressed it will be pleased to see it is forgotten.

A painful scandal is about to estrange us from an old friend. Let it rest and thus preserve our love and peace of mind.

A suspicious look is on the point of cooling our affection. Let it rest. Our look of trust will restore confidence. . . .

Imagine: we who are so careful to remove the briars from our path for fear they should wound us take pleasure in collecting and piercing our hearts with the thorns that meet us in our daily encounters with one another. How childish and unreasonable we are!

XXVI

Of all the means placed by God within our reach whereby we may lead souls to Him, there is one more blessed than all others: intercessory prayer.

*   *   *

How often in the presence of one deeply loved, but estranged from God, the heart of mother or wife has felt a sudden impulse to say an earnest word, propose an act of devotion, to paint in glowing colors the blessings of faith, and the happiness of virtue . . . and she has stopped, deterred by an irresistible fear of how the words may be received. She says to herself, *Tomorrow I shall be braver.*

*   *   *

Poor mother! Poor wife! Go and tell to your Heavenly Father everything you would like to, but dare not say to the loved one who gives you so much pain.

Lay that soul before the Lord as long ago they laid the paralytic man who could not, or perhaps would not, be led to him.

Plead for him with the long–suffering Savior as you would plead with an earthly master on whom depended all his future welfare, and say to the Savior simply, "Lord, have patience with him yet a little longer."

◆　◆　◆　◆　◆

Tell God of all your concerns, your discouragements, the means you have tried for success. Ask him to teach you what to say and how to act. One sentence learned of God in prayer will do more for the conversion of a soul than all our poor human endeavors. That sentence will escape our lips involuntarily. We may not remember that we have said it, but it will sink deep into the heart, making a lasting impression and silently fulfill its mission.

◆　◆　◆

You are, perhaps, surprised after many years to see such poor results. Oh, how little can you judge!

Do you know what you have gained? In the first place, time. Often a physical impossibility to sin, which you may attribute to chance, is in reality the work of Providence. Is it nothing, one sin the less, in the life of an immortal soul? . . . Then arises a vague uneasiness that will soon allow no rest, along with a confidence that may enable you to sympathize and more freely perform religious acts. You no longer see the contemptuous smile at your acts of devotion. Is all this nothing?

Ah, if while on your knees, praying for the one you long to have reconciled to God, you could but see what is happening in his soul—the wrestlings, the remorse he strives vainly to stifle. If you could see the work of the Holy Spirit in the heart, gently, but firmly triumphing over the will, how earnestly, how incessantly, would you continue to pray!

Only have patience to wait and perseverance to not grow weary. It is the lack of patience that often makes us demanding toward those we desire to help.

More haste, less speed, is an old saying. The more demanding we are, the less likely we are to succeed.

Men like to act freely and to have the beneficial result of their actions.

It is because we have not learned to persevere that the work seems never to progress.

Have courage then! The ground may seem too dry for cultivation, but each prayer will be as a drop of water. The marble may be very hard, but each prayer is like the hammer's stroke that wears away its roughness.

XXVII

The sweet peace of God bears the outward sign of patience.

When the Holy Spirit dwells within us, everything seems bright.

Everything may not be exactly as we would wish, but we accept all with good grace. For instance, some change in our household or way of living upsets us. If God is with us, He will whisper, "Yield cheerfully your will—in a little while all will be forgotten."

Some command or unpleasant task wounds our pride. If God is with us, he will say to us, "Be submissive, and I will come to your aid."

We may dislike a certain neighborhood. The people there may be offensive to us, and we are about to become repulsed. God will tell us to continue to be gracious and smiling, for he will repay the little annoyances we may experience. If you can discern in whom God's Spirit dwells, watch that person and notice whether you ever hear him complain.

XXVIII
I Want to Be Holy

Heavenly Father, aid thy child who longs to become holy!

But then, I must be patient in suffering. Let me be forgotten and even be pleased at feeling myself set aside.

Never mind! I am resolved. I wish to be holy!

But I must never excuse myself, never be impatient, never be in a bad mood.

Never mind! I am resolved. I wish to be holy!

Then I must continually control my feelings, submitting my will always to that of my superiors, never contentious and never moody, always finishing every job begun in spite of dislike or lack of interest.

Never mind! I am resolved. I wish to be holy!

But then I must be always loving toward all around me, loving them and helping them to the utmost of my power although it may cause me trouble.

Never mind! I am resolved. I wish to be holy!

But I must constantly strive against the cowardice, laziness, and pride of my nature; renouncing the world, the vanity that pleases, the sensuality that I love, the hate that makes me avoid those I do not like.

Never mind! I am resolved. I still wish to be holy!

Then I shall have to experience long hours of weariness, sadness, and discontent. I shall often feel lonely and discouraged.

Never mind! I am resolved. I wish to be holy! For then I shall have you always with me, ever near me. Lord, help me, for I want to be holy!

How to Become Holy

Oh, it is quite easy if I fulfill every duty to the best of my ability. Many who had no more to do than I have become saints.

One day is the same as another. Prayer, worldly business, calls to be devout, loving, and faithful: these are the duties that each hour brings in its turn, and if I am faithful in their fulfillment, God will be always ready to help me, and then what signifies a little weariness, pain, or misfortune?

* * *

The Consecration of Daily Duties

I will perform them as in God's sight, conscious that he is present and smiling on my efforts.

I will perform each as if I had but one to accomplish, striving to render it as perfect as possible.

I will fulfill each duty as if on that one alone depended my devotion.

Motives for Making Holy My Actions

God expects me to honor him by that action.

God has attached a special blessing to that action and awaits its fulfillment to bestow it.

God notes each action. At the judgment, I must give an account of all of them.

God will see that I love him if I strive to fulfill every duty in spite of my weariness and trouble.

I honor God by this action, and I, poor, weak, sinful child, am allowed to glorify him in place of those who blaspheme and rebel against his divine will.

XXIX

They say there is nothing that communicates itself so quickly among the members of a family as an expression of coldness or discontent on the face of one of its members; it is like the frost that chills us. This is not altogether true. There is something that is communicated with equal rapidity, and greater force—that is a smiling face, the beaming countenance and the happy heart.

XXX
Little Worries

There is not a day in our lives that we are not distressed by one of those numberless little worries that meet us at every step and that are inevitable. The wound made may not be deep, but the constant pricks each day renewed, embitter the character, destroy peace, create anxiety, and make family life, which otherwise would be so sweet and peaceful, almost unendurable.

Life is full of these little miseries. Each hour brings with it its own trouble.

Here are some of the little worries.

An impatient word escapes our lips in the presence of someone in whose opinion we would like to stand well.

An employee does his work badly, annoys us by his slowness, irritates us by his thoughtlessness, and his awkward blunders make us blush.

A giddy child in its clumsiness breaks something of value or that we treasure on account of its sentimental value. We are charged with a task of importance, and our forgetfulness makes us appear uncourteous, perhaps ungrateful. Someone we live with is constantly finding fault, nothing pleases him. If, when night comes, we find we have not experienced these little worries, then we ought to be grateful to God. Each of these and many more are liable to befall us every day of our lives.

How to Bear Little Worries

In the first place, expect them. Make them the subject of our morning prayers and say to ourselves, *Here is my daily cross, do I accept willingly?* Of course, for it is God who sends it. After all . . . these little troubles, looked at calmly, what are they? Thank God if there were never any worse!

Secondly, we must be prepared for them. You know, if you wish to break the force of a blow falling on you, you naturally bend the body. So let us act with regard to our souls.

Accustom yourself, wrote a pious author, to submit with a sweet attitude, not only to what is required (that is your duty), but to the simple wishes of those who surround you and the accidents that may intervene. You will find yourself seldom, if ever, crushed.

To bend is better than to resist what is often a little hard. To bend implies a certain outward sweetness, that yields all constraint, sacrificing our own wishes, even in holy things, when they tend to cause disagreements in the family circle.

Submission often implies complete resignation to all that God permits. The soul that resists feels the weight of trouble. The soul that yields scarcely perceives it.

Blessed are those docile ones. They are those whom God selects to work for Him.

XXXI
To Obtain Peace

Approach Christ in worship, oh restless soul in search of
peace, and humbly kneeling there pour forth bravely, slowly,
and with sincere desire, the following prayer:

Oh, Jesus. Gentle and humble of heart, hear me!
From the desire of being esteemed,
From the desire of being loved,
From the desire to be sought,
Deliver me, Jesus
From the desire to be mourned,
From the desire of praise,
From the desire of preference,
From the desire of influence,
From the desire of approval,
From the desire of authority,
From the fear of humiliation,
From the fear of being despised,
From the fear of repulse,
From the fear of a malicious lie,
From the fear of oblivion,
From the fear of ridicule,
From the fear of injury,
From the fear of suspicion,
Deliver me, Jesus.
That others may be loved more than myself,
Jesus grant this desire.
That others may be more highly esteemed,
That others may grow and increase in honor, and I decrease,
Jesus, grant me to desire it.

◆　◆　◆　◆　◆

That others may be used, and I set aside,
Jesus, grant me to desire this.
That others may attract the praise, and myself be forgotten,
That others may be preferred in all,
Grant me the utmost holiness of which I am capable, then let
others be holier than myself. Jesus, grant me to desire it!

Oh, if God hears, and hear he surely will if your prayer has been sincere, what joy in your heart, what peace on your face, and what sweetness will fill your whole life!

More than half one's troubles arise from an exaggerated idea of one's own importance and the efforts we make to increase our position in the world. Lacordaire says, "The sweetest thing on earth is to be forgotten by all, with the exception of those who love us. All else brings more trouble than joy, and as soon as we have completed our task here and fulfilled our mission, the best thing for us to do is to disappear altogether."

◆　◆　◆

Let us each cultivate carefully and joyously the portion of soil God has committed to our care. Let us never be hindered or distracted by ambitious thoughts that we could do better or a false zeal tempting us to forsake our daily task with the vain desire to surpass our neighbors. . . . Let this one thought occupy our minds. To do well what is given us to do, for this is all that God requires at our hands. It may be summed up in four words: simply, zealously, cheerfully, and completely.

Then if we are slighted, misunderstood, maligned, or per-secuted, what does it matter? These injuries will pass away. The peace and love of God will remain with us forever as the reward of our faith and patience. The love of God! Who can describe all the joy, strength, and consolation it reveals?

Never has human love, in its brightest dreams, been able to form any idea of the sweetness the love of God imparts to the soul and that is brought still nearer to us in prayer. I can well understand the words of a loving soul, "With heaven so near, and daily communion with our God, how can we ever complain or worry!"

XXXII
Our Father Which Art in Heaven

Oh, Jesus! It is you who asks me to say, Father! My Father! Oh, how that name rejoices my heart! My Father! I can no longer feel alone, and whatever may happen to me this day, I feel I am protected, comforted, and beloved.

Jesus, let me dwell on the sweetness of those words. My Father, I need not lift my eyes to heaven, You are within me, and where you dwell heaven must be.

* * * * *

Yes, heaven is within me! Heaven with all its peace and love, and if I keep free from guile this day, my day will be one of heavenly joy with the privilege of suffering for you.

* * *

Hallowed Be Your Name

To honor your name, O Lord, is to pronounce it with reverence and awe.

Today I will pray fervently and try to realize your presence, your goodness, and your love. My heart shall be a sanctuary into which nothing shall penetrate that could be displeasing to You.

To honor your name is to call on it fervently, to have it constantly on my lips. Above all before taking an important step when there are difficulties to be overcome, I will softly whisper the invocation, which is the secret of all holy living! "Jesus, meek and humble of heart, have pity on me."

* * *

Your Kingdom Come

Oh, Jesus, your kingdom is within my heart. Reign there in all your sovereignty and power. Reign there absolutely!

My King! What do you require of me today? Your commandments—my rule of life, my daily duties—these are your commands that I will promise to obey. More than that, I will regard all in authority over me as your ambassadors, speaking to me in your name. What matters the tone, or the harshness of the order?

What does it signify if some unexpected command upsets all my previous plans? It is your voice I hear, you Lord, whom I will obey always and in all things.

Thy kingdom is also in the hearts of others. There would I see you reigning. Then to whom can I speak of you this day? What counsels can I give? What moments may I seize in which without wounding their feelings or parading my zeal, I may be allowed to speak a few words of piety? Lord, let me have the opportunity to help another to love you!

❖ ❖ ❖

Your Will Be Done on Earth as It Is in Heaven

Yes! Yes! Your will be done! Your sweet all-perfect will! What will you send me today?

Humiliation? Provocation? Sufferings? A fresh breaking of the heart? A disappointment? Shall I see myself misjudged, falsely suspected, despised? I accept beforehand, all that you send me, and if through weakness I weep, let it to be so. If I complain, check me. If I am angry, correct me. If I am hope-less, encourage me.

Yes! Yes! Let your sweet and holy will be done!

Even, oh Lord, if to glorify you I must be humiliated, suf-fering, useless and forsaken, still, Lord, do not hold back your hand. I am wholly yours.

* * *

Give Us This Day Our Daily Bread

How blessed, oh Lord, to depend only on you. Look at me, your child, waiting with outstretched hand to receive benefits.

Grant me my physical blessings: clothing, nourishment, shelter . . . but not too much of anything. And let me have the happiness of sharing my blessings with those poorer than I am today. Grant me the blessing of intelligence that I may read or hear one of those golden counsels that elevate my soul and lend wings to the thoughts.

Grant me the loving heart, oh my Father, that I may feel for a moment how I love you and your love toward me. Let me sacrifice myself for the welfare of another. Give me the

Bread of Life. I have just received it, Lord! Grant me again that great blessing.

And then, give all these blessings, to those I love, and to those who love me!

✦ ✦ ✦

Forgive Us Our Trespasses, as We Forgive Those That Trespass Against Us

When I pronounce the word of pardon, what a weight seems lifted from my heart!

I will not only banish every feeling of hatred, I will disregard every painful memory. Oh God, if you forgive me as I forgive others, what mercy for me!

You see, I bear no malice, and I forget all injuries. . . .

I have been offended by words, I forget them. By actions, I forget them. By omissions, thoughts, desires, they are all forgotten.

Oh God, in all these ways I have offended you, and you will forget, even as I have forgotten.

I will be very merciful, so that you may have mercy on me.

Lead Us Not into Temptation, but Deliver Us from Evil.

Now as I leave your altar, I go to encounter temptation.

Oh Savior, help me, keep me, and warn me of my danger!

Let me avoid all occasions of evil, and if by weakness or temptation I am led into paths of sin and I fall, oh, rescue me speedily that I may fall upon my knees, confessing my sin and begging pardon.

Sin: this is the evil from which I beg you to deliver me. Other troubles that may happen, I accept—they are sent to try me and to purify and come from you. But sin . . . I have no pleasure in it!

Oh! When in the hour of temptation I fall away, Lord, hearken to the cry that I now raise to you in all sincerity. I desire it not! It is not my will! I go from your presence, but, Jesus, you are with me. In work, in prayer, in suffering—let all be done in you!

XXXIII

"Mother," asked a child, "since nothing is ever lost, where do all our thoughts go?"

"To God," answered the mother, gravely, "who remembers them forever."

"Forever!" said the child. He bent his head and, drawing closer to his mother, murmured, "I am frightened!"

Which of us have not felt the same?

XXXIV

One more solemn thought. How old are you? Nineteen. Have you reckoned the number of minutes that have elapsed since your birth? The number is startling: 9,333,200 . . . Each of those minutes has flown to God. God has examined them, and weighed them, and for them you must give account.

Each minute bears its own imprint (as a coin bears the imprint of the Sovereign) and only those marked with the image of God will help you for eternity.

Does not this thought make you tremble?

"I never could understand," writes Guerin, "the feeling of security some have that their works must find favor with God. As if our duties were confined to the narrow limits of this little world. To be a good son, statesman, or brother, is not all that is required of us. God demands far more than this, from those for whom He has destined a crown of glory hereafter."

XXXV

One great characteristic of holiness is never to be demanding, never to complain.

Each complaint drags us down a degree in our upward course.

By complaining, I do not mean the simple imparting of our troubles to others.

Complaint always tastes of a bad temper and a slightly vindictive spirit.

◆   ◆   ◆

The saints were never demanding.

Contented with their lot, they never desired anything that was withheld from them.

"I have asked," said a holy soul, "for something I thought needful. They have forgotten to answer me or perhaps would not give it. Why should I be upset? If it were really necessary, God would quickly provide means to obtain it." How few could enter into this feeling, and yet it is but the echo of Christ's own words, "Your Father in heaven knoweth that ye have need of all these things."

XXXVI

Joy in life is like oil in a lamp. When the oil gets low, the wick is consumed, emitting a black vapor and sending forth only a dim glow, which does not give light.

A life without joy passes away unprofitably, shedding around it only gloom and sorrow.

If every morning in a simple prayer, in those fifteen minutes' meditation (which only seems hard when we do not practice it), we open our hearts to God as we open our windows to the sun and air, God would fill it with that calm sweet joy, which elevates the soul, preventing it from feeling the weight of troubles and making it overflow with kindness.

But joy does not mean laughter, witty sayings, or a quick, witty reply. It is habitual serenity.

Through a clear atmosphere, we can always see the sky. It seems so light and clean.

A serene sky is always pure. Clouds may pass across it, but they do not stain it.

So is it with the heart that early in the morning opens to receive God's peace.

XXXVII

"You are never in a bad mood," was once said to a woman well known to suffer many trials at home. "Is it that you do not feel the injustice, the annoyances?" "I feel them as much as you do," she replied, "but they do not hurt me." "You have then some special remedy?" "Yes, for the frustrations caused by people, I have affection. For those of circumstances, I have prayer. And over every wound that bleeds, I whisper the words, 'Thy will be done.'"

XXXVIII
My Daily Cross

If I have no cross to bear today, I shall not advance heavenwards. A cross (that is anything that disturbs our peace) is the spur that stimulates, and without which we should most likely remain stationary, blinded with empty vanities and sinking deeper into sin.

A cross helps us onward in spite of our apathy and resistance. To lie quietly on a bed of down may seem a very sweet existence, but pleasant ease and rest are not the lot of a Christian. If he would mount higher and higher it must be by a rough road.

* * * * *

Alas, for those who have no daily cross!

Alas, for those who complain and resist it!

What will be my cross today?

Perhaps that person with whom providence has placed me and whom I dislike. Whose look of disdain humiliates me. Whose slowness worries me. Who makes me jealous by being more loved, more successful than I am. Whose chatter and lightheartedness, and even her very attentions to me, annoy me.

Or it may be that person, whom I think has quarrelled with me, and my imagination makes me believe myself watched, criticized, and turned into ridicule.

She is always with me. All my efforts to get away are frustrated. By some mysterious power, she is always present, always near.

* * *

This is my heaviest cross. The rest are light in comparison. Circumstances change, temptations diminish, and troubles lessen, but those people who trouble or offend us are an ever-present source of irritation.

How to Bear This Daily Cross

Never manifest in any way the weariness, the dislike, or the involuntary shudder that her presence produces. I force myself to render her some little service. Never mind if she never knows it. It is between God and myself. Try and say a little good every day of her talents, her character, and her tact, for there is all that to be found in her. Pray earnestly for her, even asking God to help me to love her and to give her to me.

Dear companion, blessed messenger of God's mercy, you are, without knowing it, the means for my sanctification, and I will not be ungrateful!

Yes! Though the exterior be rude and repulsive, yet to you I owe it, that I am kept from greater sin. You, against whom my whole nature rebels . . . how I ought to love you!

XXXIX

Who is anxious for a loved one's eternal welfare?

We concern ourselves for their success and their prosperity. We ask God to keep them from harm and misfortune. We try to start them well in the world, to make them of reputation and to give them pleasure.

To spare them trouble, we sacrifice our own ease and enjoyment.

Oh, that is all very beautiful, very right. But what should we do for the soul?

Do we pray to God that this soul may become humble, pure, and devoted?

Do we take as much pains to procure for him the little devotional book, which will really help him, as we should to obtain a temporary pleasure?

Do we help him unseen toward that act of charity, humiliation, or self-sacrifice? Have we courage not to spare the soul the trial that we know will purify?

Does it seem too hard for you?

Ah, then you do not know what real love is. Does not God love us? Yet, God lets us suffer, even sends the suffering.

Love is given us, to help us onwards, nearer to God. The most blessed is that which draws us nearest to Him. In proportion as it leads to God, we realize its blessedness.

The essence of true love is not its tenderness, but its strength, power of endurance, its purity, and its self-renunciation.

The mistake we make is when we seek to be loved instead of loving. What makes us cowardly is the fear of losing that love.

Never forget this: a selfish heart desires love for itself; a Christian heart delights to love without return.

XL

To learn never to waste our time is perhaps one of the most difficult virtues to acquire.

A well-spent day is a source of pleasure. To be constantly employed and never asking, "What shall I do?" is the secret of much goodness and happiness.

Begin then promptly, act decisively, and persevere. If interrupted, be friendly and return to the work unruffled, finishing it carefully. These will be the signs of a virtuous soul.

XLI

Are you full of peace?
Pray! Prayer will preserve it to you.
Are you tempted?
Pray! Prayer will sustain you.
Have you fallen?
Pray! Prayer will raise you.
Are you discouraged?
Pray! Prayer will reassure and comfort you.

XLII

The young are seldom patient because they so little understand the frailties of human nature.

Oh, if you could only witness the terrible struggles passing in the heart of that friend whose spirit annoys you, whose indecision provokes you, and whose faults sometimes even make you blush.

Oh, if you saw the tears that are shed in secret and the distress felt against self, perhaps on your account, you would indeed pity him. Love him! Make allowances for him and never let him feel that you know his failings.

To make any one believe he is good is to help him, almost in spite of himself, to become so.

* * *

Forgiveness is even more than tolerance; it is excusing, putting always the best point of view on everything, above all, never showing that some action has wounded us by speaking of anyone who has provoked us thus: "She did not think, else she would have acted differently. She never meant to hurt me, she loves me too much. She was perhaps unable to do otherwise, and yet suffers at the thought of having displeased me."

For a wounded heart, no balm is so effective as forgiveness.

To forgive is to forget every night the little annoyances of the past day. To say every morning, "Today I shall be braver and calmer than yesterday." Forgiveness sometimes even leads us to detect in ourselves a small lack of good nature, pride, and lack of love.

To forgive is not only to excuse, but to meet halfway with an extended hand those who timidly ask for pardon.

XLIII

My friend, do you know why the work you accomplish fails either to give pleasure to yourself or others?

It is because it is not cheerfully done and therefore appears done unwillingly.

A joyous heart amid our work gives to duty a brilliancy that charms the eyes of others, while it prevents those who cannot perform it equally well from feeling wounded.

Joy with us is like a lever by which we lift the weights that without its help would crush us.

A workman once said, "If I were to leave off singing, I should be quite unequal to my task."

◆ ◆ ◆ ◆ ◆

Then sing always. Let your heart sing as in its earliest years.

The refrain of the heart, which perhaps never passes the lips, but which echoes in heaven, is this sentence: "I love, and I am loved."

XLIV

What regret we sometimes feel after the death or departure of a friend at never having shown him the respect and the gratitude we felt toward him, and how from the depths of our hearts we are filled with tenderness and affection for him!

It may have been that at times we could not speak because we thought too much of how to say it.

Another time, we lost the opportunity because we were always avoiding it. Deep devotion is sometimes a little erratic. We are always afraid of doing too little or doing it badly or at the wrong time.

Often the expressions of affection are held back because we think we could show it in some better way. We put off until brighter days the dreams we cherished, the sweet yearning to open the heart to the loved ones to let them see for once what a large place they fill there.

❖　❖　❖　❖　❖

Alas, the days fly past. Suddenly comes death or, sadder still, separation without hope of return, leaving the bitter thought, "Others will show them better than I have done, how dear, how valued they are." Ah, when we can be loving today, never let us say, "I will love tomorrow." When we have the opportunity of being grateful, never put off, for one hour, the proof of our gratitude!

CONCLUSION

Lacordaire, in preparing for a retreat in the country, said he only required for his realization of a dream of happiness and solitude three things: God, a friend, and books.

God. We never fail to find him when we are pure, holy, and fulfilling hourly our duty.

A Friend. Responds always to the heart's call, if only that heart be loving and devoted.

Books. Oh, if only this little book of gold dust might be allowed to be one of those that are carried away, far from the world's turmoil, and read to gain a little help and peace!

It will take up so little room!

PART TWO
Gold Dust

I
The Friendly Whisper

Under this title we begin a series of short counsels for each day of the week that will be as a friendly whisper or the voice of the Spirit of God, often inspiring, some requiring good action, some self-denial, and some a small sacrifice.

We recommend that this book be placed on the desk or nightstand, beside the book you most frequently turn to or wherever it is most likely to catch the eye. What is so often the one thing lacking in some devout person devoted to doing good? Simply to be reminded of it.

M O N D A Y
Charity

Be good-natured, giving, and keeping up a cheerful expression and attitude, even when alone, so that when you experience others' clumsiness and gruff, rude manners, you let them pass without notice.

When wishes contrary to your own win out, yield without a bad attitude or even showing your effort. You will give pleasure, and as a result, be pleased yourself.

Try to please, to comfort, to amuse, to give, to thank, to help. That is all in itself so good!

Try and do some good to the souls of others with an earnest word, some encouragement, or a prayer softly breathed.

Overcome your dislike of certain persons. Do not avoid them; on the contrary, go and meet them. God goes before you.

Be courteous even to the troublesome individual who is always in your way. God sends him to you.

Forgive at once. Do you believe that harm was intended? If so, is it not better to forgive?

Do not refuse your financial contributions and charitable giving. Let your motives be pure, and in giving, give as to God.

* * * * *

Do not judge the guilty harshly. Pity and pray for them.

Why imagine evil intentions against yourself? Cannot you see how the thought troubles and disturbs you?

Check the sarcastic smile hovering about your lips. You will grieve the one who is the object of it. Why cause anyone pain?

Lend yourself to all. God will not allow you to be taken advantage of if you are prompted by the spirit of love.

* * *

TUESDAY
The Divine Presence

Never separate yourself from God. How sweet it is to live always near those who love us!

You cannot see God, but he is there, just as if some friend were separated from you by a curtain, which does not prevent his seeing you and may at any moment unfold and disclose him to your view.

When the soul is unstained by sin, and if we remain still and calm, we can feel God's presence in the heart just as we feel daylight penetrating a room. We may not be always conscious of this presence, but almost imperceptibly it influences all our actions. Oh, however heavy may be the burden you have to bear, does it not at once become light beneath the gaze of the Father's eye?

The thought of God is never wearisome. Why not always cherish it? Go on without trembling, beneath the eye of God, never fearing to smile, love, hope, and enjoy all that makes life sweet.

God rejoices in our pleasures as a mother in the joys of her child.

What is contrary to God's will grieves him and does you harm. That alone you should fear. The thought will also stain your soul, the wish trouble your heart. That unwholesome action will weaken your intellect and destroy your peace.

Never long for what God sees fit to deny.

God, beside you, will help you repair your mistakes and provide means whereby you may make amends for that sinful action. He will, by one more virtuous, wipe away the tears caused by some undeserved reprimand or unkind word.

You have only to close your eyes for a moment, examine yourself, and softly murmur, "Lord, help me!"

Can you not hear God's voice speaking to you? When he says, "Bear this, I am here to aid you," will you refuse?

He says, "Continue another half-hour the work that wearies you." And you would stop?

He says, "Do not do that." And you do it?

He says, "Let us walk together the path of obedience." And you answer no?

WEDNESDAY
Self-Denial

Do not be afraid of that word *denial*. To you, perhaps, it only means, weariness, restraint, or boredom.

But it means also love, perfection, and sanctification.

Who cannot deny self, cannot love.
Who cannot deny self, cannot become perfect.
Who cannot deny self, cannot be made holy.

Self-denial means devotion to our duty, going on with it in spite of difficulties, disgust, boredom, or lack of success.

Self-denial is self-sacrifice in whatever form it presents itself: prayer, labor, love . . . all that would be an obstacle not merely to its accomplishment, but its perfection.

Self-denial is to root out all that burdens the heart, all that obstructs the free action of the Holy Spirit within. Longings after an imaginary perfection or well-being and unreal sentiments that trouble us in prayer, in work, or in slumber may fascinate us, but their result destroys all real application.

* * * * *

Self–denial is to resist all the temptations of the senses that would only give pleasure to self and satisfy the conscience by whispering, "It is no sin."

Self–denial is the destroying, even at the risk of much pain and sacrifice, all in our heart, mind, and imagination that could be displeasing to God.

Self–denial is not one single action that when once accomplished brings relief. It means a constant sacrifice, restraint, resisting, and separating at each hour and each moment during our whole life.

But is not this a worry and a continual torment? No, not if the motivation is love or godly fear. . . .

Do you consider it a trouble when you make yourself less comfortable to make room for a friend who visits you?

Well, there are times when God would make you aware of his presence. He is with you, and to retain him, who is all purity, will you not be more modest in your behavior?

If you would receive him into your heart, will you not make room for him by rooting out that affection he has pointed out to you as dangerous, or that interest, that desire, that worldly sensual attachment?

Oh, if you only *really* loved.

Would you call *torture* or *constraint* the energy with which you shatter some poisoned cup that you were almost enticed to drink?

◆　◆　◆　◆　◆

Well, when encountering the attractive enjoyment—the material delight, which might lead you astray, or the voice that would allure you from your duty for a moment—then, when conscience whispers, *Beware,* would you be cowardly?

Sadly, it is slowly and surely that the stream carries on to destruction the blossom that has fallen into its current.

It is little by little that pleasure leads on to sin the heart that lets itself be lulled by its charms.

◆　◆　◆

THURSDAY
Submission

As soon as you awake in the morning, try and realize God stretching forth his hand toward you, saying, *Do you really desire that I should watch over you this day?* Lift up your hands toward this kind Father and say to him, "Yes. Yes, lead me, guide me, love me. I will be very submissive!"

Beneath God's protecting hand, is it possible that you can be sorrowful, fearful, or unhappy?

No, God will allow no suffering, no trial above what you are able to bear.

Then pass through the day, quietly and calmly, even as when a little child, you had your mother always beside you.

* * * * *

You need only be careful about one thing—*never to displease* God—and you will see how lovingly God will direct all that concerns you: material interests, emotions, or worldly cares. You will be astonished at the sudden enlightenment that will come to you and the wondrous peace that will result from your labor and your toil.

Then welcome trial, sickness, boredom, wants, or injustice . . . all of it can only come directed by God's hand and will wound the soul only in order to cleanse some spot within.

Would your mother have given you a bitter dose, merely for the sake of causing suffering?

If your duty is hard, owing either to its difficulty or the distaste you feel towards it, lift your heart to God and say: "Lord, help me," then go on with it even though you seem to do it imperfectly.

Should one of those moments of vague doubts that leave the soul as if it were in complete darkness come to overwhelm you, call on God, as a child in terror cries out to its mother.

If you have sinned, even then be not afraid of the merciful God, but with eyes full of tears, say to him, "Pardon me," and add softly, "chastise me soon, O Lord!"

Yes, yes, dear one, be always at peace, going on quietly with your daily duties . . . more than that, be always joyous.

❖   ❖   ❖   ❖   ❖

And why not?

You who no longer have a mother to love you, and yet crave for love, God will be as a mother. You who have no brother to help you, and have so much need of support, God will be your brother. You who have no friends to comfort you, and stand so much in need of consolation, God will be your friend.

Preserve always the *childlike simplicity,* which goes directly to God, and speak to him as you would speak to your mother.

Keep that open confidence that tells him your projects, troubles, and joys as you tell them to a brother.

Cherish those loving words that speak of all the happiness you feel, living in dependence on him and trusting in his love just as you would a childhood friend.

Keep the generous heart of childhood that gives all you have to God. Let him freely take whatever he pleases, all within and around you. Want only what he wants, desiring only what is in accordance with his will, and finding nothing impossible that he commands.

Do you not feel something soothing and consoling in these thoughts? The longer you live, the better you will understand that true happiness is only to be found in a life devoted to God and given up entirely to his guidance.

* * * * *

No! No one can harm you, unless it be God's will, and if he allows it, be patient and humble. Weep if your heart is broken, but love always and wait . . . the trial will pass away, but God will remain yours for ever.

* * *

FRIDAY
Prayer

Oh, if you only knew what it is to pray! Oh, if God would only give you the grace to love prayer. What peace to your soul! What love in your heart! What joy would shine in your countenance, even though the tears streamed from your eyes!

Prayer: As the first cry escapes the lips, it indicates to God that someone would speak to him, and God, so good and gracious, is ever ready to listen. With all reverence we say it with the prompt attention of a faithful servant. He reveals himself to the soul, with unspeakable love, and says to it, "Behold me, you have called me, what do you desire of me?"

To pray is to remain, so long as our prayer lasts, in the presence of God with the certainty that we can never weary him no matter what may be the subject of our prayer . . . or at those times when we are speechless, and as in the case of the good peasant quoted by the Cure d'Ars, we are content to place ourselves before God with only the memory of his presence.

* * * * *

To pray is to act toward God as the child does to his mother; or the poor man toward the rich, eager to do him good; or the friend toward his friend who longs to show him affection.

Prayer is the key to all celestial treasures; by it we penetrate into the midst of all the joy, strength, mercy, and goodness divine, and we receive our well-being from all around us as the sponge plunged into the ocean absorbs without effort the water that surrounds it . . . this joy, strength, mercy and goodness become our own.

Oh, yes! If you knew how to pray and loved prayer, how good, useful, fruitful, and praiseworthy would be your life.

Nothing so elevates the soul as prayer.

God, descending to the soul, raises it with him to the regions of light and love; and then the prayer finished, the soul returns to its daily duties with a more enlightened mind and a more earnest will. It is filled with radiance divine and shines with its abundance on all who approach.

If you would succeed in your study with the success that sanctifies, pray before beginning.

If you would succeed in your interaction with others, pray before becoming intimate.

Nothing so smooths and sweetens life as *prayer*.

There is the *solitary prayer*, when the soul, isolated from all creatures and alone with God, feels this way toward him:

"God and I"—God to love, I to adore, praise, glorify, and thank. God to bestow, I to humbly receive, renounce, ask, hope, and submit!

Ah, who can tell all that passes between the soul and its God!

There is the *united prayer* of two friends, bound together by a holy friendship, their desires and thoughts are one, and as one they present themselves before God, crying, "Have mercy on me!"

There is the prayer of two hearts separated by distance, made at the same hour in the same words. Soothing prayer each day reunites those two sad hearts torn by the agony of parting, and who, in God's presence strengthened with the same Holy Spirit, recover courage to tread the road to heaven, each in its appointed region.

Then there is *public prayer* that has the special promise of God's presence. Prayer is so comforting to the feeble, guilty soul, who can cry in very truth, "My prayer ascends to God, supported by the prayers of others."

Oh, if you knew how to pray and loved prayer, how happy and fruitful your life would be!

S A T U R D A Y
Earnestness

You love God do you not, dear one, whom God surrounds with so much affection?

Yes! Yes, I love him!

And how do you prove to him your love?

I keep myself pure and innocent so that his eye falling on me may never see anything that displeases him. I keep myself calm and quiet and force myself to smile that he may see I am contented.

That is right, but that is not enough.

I think often of how much I owe him and apply myself diligently to the work he has given me to do. I bear patiently with those I dislike and with troubles that irritate me. When I am weak I call on him, when timid I draw near to him, and when sinful I ask forgiveness and strive to do my duty more faithfully.

That is right, but that is not enough.

I give myself to the requests of others. I am as a slave to those who need me and take care never to judge any one harshly.

That is right, but still it is not enough.

* * * * *

Ah, then what more can I do, good Spirit of God who is addressing me? What can I do to show my love to God?

Devote yourself to doing good to the souls of others!

Oh, if you knew how it pleases God to see you serving them! It is like the joy of a mother, every time she sees some—one helping her child.

How thankful she is to those who nursed it in sickness; spared it pain; showed it some token of affection, a counsel, a warning; that gave it pleasure by a kind word, a plaything, or a smile.

All this you may do in that circle, more or less extended, in which you live.

Leave to God's minister, if you will, the work of convert—ing souls, and limit your efforts to doing good by bringing yourself into contact with them.

To do so means to sweetly, unconsciously, softly speak to them of God, carry them to God, and lead them to God.

This may be done by gently and tenderly, by inference as it were, speaking to them of God, and by doing so leading them toward him, bringing them into contact with him.

Hearts are drawn together by talking of their kindred pursuits, souls by speaking of heavenly things.

It is not necessary for this purpose, to pronounce the name of God. It will be enough that the words will lift the soul beyond this material world, and its sensual enjoyments,

* * * * *

and raise them upwards to that supernatural atmosphere necessary to the real life.

Speak of the happiness of devotion, the charm of purity, the blessing of the few minutes meditation at the feet of Jesus, the peace acquired by complete resignation to providence, and the sweetness of a life spent beneath God's fatherly eye, the comfort the thought of heaven brings in the midst of trouble, the hope of the meeting again above, and the certainty of eternal happiness. This is doing good to others, drawing them nearer to God, and teaching them more and more of his holiness.

Limit your efforts to this.

* * *

SUNDAY
Sympathy

Welcome with joy each week the day that God has called his day.

To each day of the week God has given its special mission, its share of pleasure and of pain necessary to purify and strengthen and prepare us for eternity.

But *Sunday* is a day of love.

On Saturday we lay aside our garments faded and stained by toil and on Sunday we dress ourselves in garments, not only fresher, but finer.

・　　・　　・　　・　　・

Why not prepare the heart, even as we do the body?

During the week, has not the heart been wearied with petty strife and discontent, interests marred, and bitter words?

Then why not shake off all this that only chills affection? On Saturday let us forgive freely, shake hands warmly, embrace each other and then, peace being restored within, we await the tomorrow's awakening.

Sunday is God's day of truce for all. That day, laying aside all revenge and ill-feeling, we must be filled with tolerance, indulgence, and gratefulness.

Oh, how good for us to feel *obliged* to be reconciled, and each Sunday renews the obligation.

Let us leave no time for coldness and indifference to grow on us . . . it only produces hatred. Once that is established in the heart, how very hard it is to cast it out again. It is like a hideous cancer whose ravages no remedies can hold back. It is as the poisonous plant, that the gardener can never entirely eliminate. Only by a miracle can hatred be destroyed. At once then let us place a barrier in our hearts, against the approach of coolness, or indifference, and each Saturday night the head of the family shall thus address us: "Children, tonight we forgive, tonight we forget. Tomorrow, we begin life afresh in love one towards another."

II

"When I have sinned," wrote a pious soul, "I feel that punishment will fall on me, and, as if I could hide myself from God's eye, I *shrink* into myself. Then I pray, I pray, and the punishment not being sent, I again expand."

Punishment is like a stone threatening to crush me. *Prayer* is the hand that holds it back, while I make atonement.

Oh, how can people live peacefully, who never pray?

III
Our Dead

They are not all there, our dead. Those buried in the churchyard, beneath the grave, overshadowed by a cross, and around which the roses bloom.

There are others whom nothing can recall. They are things that belong to the *heart* alone, and there, have found a tomb.

Peace surrounds me today. Here, in my lone chamber, I will remember them. My much-loved dead. Come!

✦ ✦ ✦ ✦ ✦

✦ ✦ ✦

The first that present themselves are the sweet years of childhood, so fresh, so innocent, so happy. They were made up of loving caresses, bountiful rewards, and fearless confidence. The words, *pain, danger, and care* were unknown. Childhood brought me simple pleasure, happy days without a thought for tomorrow, and only required a little obedience from me.

Alas, they are dead . . . and what many things have they carried with them! What an emptiness they have left! Innocence, lightheartedness, simplicity no longer find a place within! Family ties, so true, so wide, so light, have all vanished!

The homely hearth, the simple reward earned by the day's hard work, maternal reprimands, forgiveness so innocently sought, so freely given, and promises of improvement, so sincere, so joyously received—is this all gone forever? Can I never recall them?

✦ ✦ ✦

The vision that follows is that of my *early devotion,* simple and full of faith, which was as some good angel overshadowing me with its snowy wings and showing me God everywhere, in all, and with all.

The good God who each day provides my daily bread.

* ❖ ❖ ❖ ❖ ❖

The God who spared my mother in sickness and relieved her when she suffered. God, who shielded me from harm, when I did right.

The God who sees all, knows all, and is omnipotent. Whom I loved with all my heart.

Alas! Faithful, simple devotion, you are dead. In innocence alone could you live!

❖ ❖ ❖

Next comes *the love of my earliest years.* Love in childhood, love in youth, so full of true, simple joy, that initiated me in the sweet pleasure of devotion, that taught me self-denial in order to give pleasure, and that destroyed all egotism by showing me the happiness of living for others.

Love of my childhood, love of my youth—so pure, so holy—on which I always reckoned when they spoke to me of trouble, loneliness, depression . . . you also are dead.

An involuntary coolness, an unfounded suspicion never cleared, a lewd joke . . . all these have destroyed that child of heaven. I knew it was tender and I cherished it, but I could not believe it to be so frail.

I could make a long list of all the dead enshrined in my heart! Oh, you who are still young, on whom God has lavished all the gifts that are lost to me—simplicity, innocence, love, devotion—guard, oh, guard these treasures, and that they may never die, place them beneath the protective shelter of *prayer.*

IV
The Spiritual Life

What a sweet life is that! The maintaining and strengthening of it has a softening influence, and it is a labor that never wearies, never deceives, but gives each day fresh cause for joy.

In the language of devotion, it is called *the inner life,* and it is our purpose to point out minutely its nature, excellence, means, and hindrances.

Let no one think the inner life is incompatible with family and social life, which is often so engaging. Just as the action of the heart maintained by the constant flow of blood in no way affects the outward movements, so is it with the life of the soul, which consists chiefly in the action of God's Holy Spirit within, that never hinders our social duties, but on the contrary is a help toward fulfilling them more calmly and more perfectly.

◆ ◆ ◆

Nature of the Inner Life

The inner life is an abiding sense of God's presence, a constant union with him.

We learn to look on the heart as the temple where God dwells, sometimes glorious as above, sometimes hidden. We act, think, speak, and fulfill all our duties as in his presence.

* * * * *

Its aim is to avoid sin and cultivate a detachment from all earthly things by a spirit of poverty. Avoid sensual pleasure through purity, pride by humility, and distraction by meditation.

As a rule, people are prejudiced against an inner life. Some are afraid of it and look on it as a life of bondage, sacrifice, and restraint. Others despise it as nothing but a great deal of trivial rules, tending only to narrow-mindedness and uselessness, and fit only for weak minds. In consequence, they are on their guard against it and avoid the books that deal with it.

They would serve God no doubt, but they will not subject themselves to the entire guidance of his Spirit. In short, it is far easier to bring a soul from a state of sin to that of grace than it is to lead a busy, active, zealous person to the hidden, contemplative life of the soul.

* * *

Excellence of the Inner Life

God dwelling within us, the life of Christ himself, when on earth, living always in his Father's Presence . . . .

It is the life of which Paul speaks when he says, "Nevertheless I live, yet not I, but Christ lives in me."

All saints must lead this life and their degree of holiness is in proportion to the perfection of their union with God.

* * * * *

Christ animates their souls, even as the soul animates the body. They own Christ as master, counselor, and guide, and nothing is done without submitting it to him and imploring his aid and approval.

Christ is their strength, their refuge, and their defender. They live in constant dependence on him, as their Father, Protector, and all-powerful King.

They are drawn to him, as the child is drawn by love and the poor by need. They let themselves be guided by him as the blind let themselves be led by the child in whom they confide. They bear all suffering that comes from him, as the sick in order to be healed bear suffering at the hands of a physician. They lean on him, as the child leans on her mother's breast.

It lifts them above the troubles and miseries of life. The whole world may seem a victim of calamities. They, too, are deprived of their goods through injustice or accident. They lose their family members through death, their friends through disloyalty or forgetfulness, their reputation and honor from slander. A serious illness deprives them of health, and their happiness is destroyed by hardness and temptations.

Ah, no doubt they will have these trials. No doubt they must shed bitter tears, but still God's peace will remain to them, the peace that passeth all understanding. They will realize God has ordered it and guided it with his hand divine, and they will be able to exclaim with joy, "You are still with us and you are all-sufficient!"

◆ ◆ ◆

Acts of the Inner Life

1. *See God.* That is to say, be always realizing his presence and feeling him near, as the friend from whom we would never be separated, in work, in prayer, in recreation, and in rest. God is not insistent, he never wearies, he is so gracious and merciful. His hand directs everything, and he will not "suffer us to be tempted above that we are able."

2. *Listen to God.* Be attentive to his counsels and his warnings. We hear his voice, in those gospel words that return to our minds in the good thoughts that suddenly dawn on us, the godly words that meet us in some book, on a sheet of paper, or falling from the lips of a preacher, a friend, or even a stranger.

3. *Speak to God.* Hold conversation with him, more with the heart than the lips, in the early morning's meditation, spontaneous prayer, or vocal prayer, and above all in personal worship and communion.

4. *Love God.* Be devoted to him and him alone. Have no affection apart from him. Restrain the love that would

estrange us from him. Lend ourselves to all out of love to him, but give ourselves to him alone.

5. *Think of God.* Rejecting whatever excludes the thought of him. Of course, we must fulfill our daily duties, accomplishing them with all the perfection of which we are capable, but they must be done as beneath the eye of God with the thought that God has commanded them, and that to do them carefully is pleasing in his sight.

◆　◆　◆

Means by Which to Attain the Inner Life

1. *Great tenderness of conscience* secured by constant, regular, and earnest confession to God is necessary, along with a hatred of all sin, imperfection, and infidelity. Calmly but resolutely flee every occasion of sin.

2. *Great purity of heart* by detachment from all earthly things, wealth, luxuries, fame, family, friends, tastes, even life itself . . . not that we need fail in love to our family and friends, but we must only let the thought of them abide in the heart, as united to the love and thought of God.

3. *Great purity of mind,* carefully excluding from it all useless, distracting thoughts as to past, present, or future; all

preoccupation over some petty employment; all desire to be known and thought well of.

4. *Great purity of action,* only undertaking what lies in the path of duty; controlling natural eagerness and activity; acting soberly with the help of the Holy Spirit; retaining the thought that by our deeds we glorify God; pausing for a moment, when passing from one occupation to another, to direct intentions correctly; and taking care to be always occupied in what is useful and beneficial.

5. *Great remembrances and self-discipline,* avoiding, as much as we can, in keeping with our social position, all diversion, bustle, and disturbance. Never allow voluntarily useless desires, looks, words, or pleasures. Placing them under the rule of reason, etiquette, edification, and love. Take care that our prayers be said slowly and carefully, articulating each word and try to feel the truth of what we are saying.

6. *Great care and accuracy* in all the ordinary actions of life, above all in the exercises of religion, leaving nothing to chance or hazard, beholding in everything God's overruling will, and saying to oneself sometimes, as the hour for such and such duty arrives, "I must hurry, God is calling me."

7. *Much interaction with God,* speaking to him with simplicity, loving him dearly, always consulting him, giving to him an account of every action, thanking him constantly, and above all, drawing near to him with joy in worship. One

great help towards such sweet fellowship with God will be found in a steady discipline in the early morning's meditation.

8. *Much love for our neighbor* because he is the much-loved child of God, praying for him, comforting, teaching, strengthening, and helping him in all difficulties.

◆ ◆ ◆

Hindrances to the Inner Life

1. *Natural activity,* always urging us on and making us too hasty in all our actions.

It shows itself:

In our projects, which it multiplies, heaps up, reforms, and upsets. It allows no rest until what it has undertaken is accomplished.

In our actions. Activity is absolutely necessary to us. We load ourselves with a thousand things beyond our duty, sometimes even contrary to it. Everything is done with impulsiveness, haste, anxiety, and impatience to see the end.

In our conversation. Activity makes us speak without thinking, interrupting rudely, reproving hastily, judging without appreciation. We speak loudly, disputing, murmuring, and losing our tempers.

In prayer. We burden ourselves with numberless prayers, repeated carelessly, without attention, and with impatience to get to the end of them. It interferes with our meditations and wearies, torments, and fatigues the mind, drying up the soul, and hindering the work of the Holy Spirit.

2. *Curiosity* lays the soul open to all external things, filling it with a thousand fancies and questionings—pleasing or annoying—absorbing the mind, and making it quite impossible to retire within oneself and be recollected. Then follow distaste, laziness, and boredom for all that resembles silence, solitude, and meditation.

Curiosity shows itself, when studies are undertaken, out of vanity and a desire to know all things, appearing clever . . . rather than the real wish to learn, in order to be useful. Curiosity shows itself in reading, when the spare time is given up to history, papers, and novels, and in *walking,* when our steps would lead us where the crowd goes to see, to know, only in order to have something to tell. In fact, it manifests itself in a thousand little actions. For instance, pressing forward with feverish haste to open a letter addressed to us, longing eagerly to see anything that presents itself, or wanting always to be the first to tell any piece of news. . . . When we forget God, he is driven from the heart, leaving it void, and then ensues that wild craving to fill up the void with anything with which we may come into contact.

* * * * *

3. *Cowardice.* God does not forbid patient, submissive pleading, but murmuring fears are displeasing to him, and he withdraws from the soul that will not lean on him. Cowardice manifests itself, when, in the trials of life, we rebel against the divine will that sends us illness, scandal, privation, or desertion. When in dryness of soul, we leave off our prayers and communion because we feel no sensible sweetness in them when we feel a sickness of the soul, that makes us uneasy and fearful that God has forsaken us.

The soul estranged from God seeks diversion in the world, but in the midst of the world, God is not to be found. When temptations come, wearied, frightened, and tormented, we wander farther and farther away from him, crying, "I am forsaken," when the trial has really been sent, in order to keep us on our guard, to prevent our becoming proud, and offering us an opportunity for showing our love.

V
The Lesson of a Daisy

I saw her from afar, poor child. She looked dreamy as she leaned against the window and held in her hand a daisy, which she was questioning by gradually pulling it to pieces. What she wanted to ascertain I cannot tell. I only heard in a low murmur, falling from her pale lips, these words: "A little, a great deal, passionately, not at all," as each petal her fingers pulled away fell fluttering at her feet.

I could see her from a distance, and I felt touched.

Poor child, why do you tell a flower the thought that troubles you? Have you no mother?

Why be anxious about the future? Have you not God to prepare it for you, as tenderly as eighteen years ago your mother prepared your cradle?

Finally, when the daisy was all but gone, when her fingers stopped at the last petal, and her lips murmured the word *little,* she dropped her head upon her arms, discouraged. Poor child, she wept!

✦ ✦ ✦

Why weep, my child? Is it because this word does not please you?

Let me, let me, in the name of the simple daisy you have just destroyed, give you the experience of my old age.

Oh, if you only knew what it costs to have much of anything!

A great deal of wit often results in spitefulness, which makes us cruel and unjust in jealousy that torments, in deception that spoils all our triumphs, and in pride that is never satisfied.

A great deal of heart causes uneasiness, which torments, pain that tears apart, grief that nearly kills . . . sometimes even the judgment is deceived.

A great deal of attractiveness, means often a consuming vanity, overwhelming deception, an insatiable desire to please, a fear of being unappreciated, a loss of peace, and a family life much neglected.

A great deal of wealth and success are the cause of luxury that causes weakness, loss of peace and quiet happiness, and loss of love, leaving only the flattery that captivates.

No, no, my child, never long for a great deal in this life, unless it be for much tolerance, much goodness.

And if it should be God's will to give you *much* of any‐thing, then, oh, pray it may never be to your condemnation!

❖ ❖ ❖

Is *passionately* the word you long for? Passionately! Oh, the harm that is done by that word! There is something in the thought of it that makes me shudder. Passionately means rap‐ture, frenzy, excess in everything.

The life that the word *passionately* describes must be a life full of risks and dangers. And, if by little short of a miracle, nothing outwardly wrong appears, the inner life must resem‐ble a palace, ravaged by fire, where the stranger sees nothing but cracked walls, blackened furniture, and drapery hanging in shreds!

My child, I would prefer for you the words *not at all*, as applied to fortune, external charms, and all that goes by the name of glory, success, and fascination in the world. I know it may seem a hard sentence, involving a continual self–denial and exacting, incessant hard labor to obtain the bare necessities of life for those we love.

But do not be afraid of it. God never leaves his creatures in absolute need. God may deprive a face of beauty, a character of being agreeable, a mind of brilliancy, but he will never take away a heart of love. With the capability of loving, he adds the power of prayer, and the promise always to listen to it and answer it.

As long as we can love and pray, life has beauty for us. Love produces devotion, and devotion brings happiness, even though we may not understand it. In prayer we feel we are beloved, and the love of God, oh, if only you knew how it compensates for the indifference of our fellow creatures!

✦   ✦   ✦

There now only remains to us the last words of the daisy, *a little!* The loving, fatherly answer God has given to your childish curiosity: *Accept it, and make it the motto of your life!*

A little. Moderation in wealth and fortune, a condition that promises the most peaceful life, free from anxiety for the

* * * * *

future, doubtless requiring daily duties, but permitting many innocent enjoyments.

A little. Moderation in our desires, contentment with what we possess, making the most of it, and repressing all vain dreams of a more brilliant position, a more extended reputation, and a more famous name.

A little. The affection of a heart devoted to duty, kindling joy in the family circle, which is composed of kindred to love, friends to cheer, poor to assist, hearts to strengthen, and sufferings to alleviate.

A little. A taste for all that is beautiful. Books, works of art, music, not making us idly dream of fame, but simply providing enjoyment for the mind—all the more special as the daily toil makes the occasions rare.

Do you see, my child, how much may lie beneath those simple words, *a little,* that the daisy gave you, and that you seem so much to despise?

Never scorn anything that seems wanting in brilliance, and remember to be really happy we must have

More *virtue* than knowledge,

More *love* than tenderness,

More *wisdom* than cleverness,

More *health* than riches,

More *rest* than profit.

VI

Each day is like a furrow lying before us. Our thoughts, desires, and actions are the seed that we drop into it each minute without seeming to perceive it. The furrow finished, we begin another, then another, and again another; each day presents a fresh one, and so on to the end of life . . . sowing, ever sowing. And all we have sown springs up, grows, and bears fruit, almost unknown to us. Even if we cast a back-ward glance we fail to recognize our work.

Behind us, angels and demons, like gleaners, gather together in sheaves all that belongs to them.

Every night their store is increased. They preserve it and at the last day will present it to their masters.

Is there not a thought in this that should make us reflect?

VII
"Learn of Me, For I Am Meek and Lowly of Heart"

This is a simple rule of life for me, requiring no more than I am able, but I feel it unites me to God, makes me more devout, more faithful to duty, more ready for death. Since I have made it my rule, it has been to me a source of consolation, enlightenment, and strength, and yet God alone knows how full of pain my life has been!

Dear friends who, like myself, long to become holy, I commend this sentence to you, in all its simplicity. Listen, for it comes from the loving heart of Jesus. It fell from his gentle lips, "Learn of me, for I am meek and lowly of heart."

A.

Be Meek

1. MEEK TOWARD GOD

Be meek toward God, living from day to day beneath his eye where all things are ordered by a divine providence.

As carefully as a mother arranges the room where her child will pass the day, does God prepare each hour that opens before me. Whatever has to be done, it is his will that I should do it. In order that it should be done well he provides the necessary time, intelligence, aptitude, and knowledge.

Whatever of suffering presents itself, he expects me to bear it, even though I may not see any reason for it. If the pain be so sharp as to call forth a cry, he gently whispers, "Courage, my child for it is my will!"

* * * * *

If anything occurs to hinder my work, anything goes contrary to my plans and projects, he has ordained it so, on purpose, because he knows that too much success would make me proud, too much ease would make me sensual, and he would teach me that the road to heaven is not *success,* but *labor and devotion.*

With such thoughts as these, all rebellion is hushed! With that peace, with what joy our work may be begun, continued, interrupted, and resumed!

With what energy we reject those enemies that assail us at every hour: idleness, haste, preoccupation, success, and lack of perseverance under difficulties!

Does the past sometimes rise up to trouble me with the thought of many years spent without God? Ah, no doubt the shame and grief are sharp and keen, but why do they need to disturb my peace of mind?

Has not God promised his pardon for his blessed Son's sake to all who truly repent and genuinely believe his holy gospel? Have I made a full acknowledgment and entire submission? And am I not willing to fulfill whatever I am advised in God's name to do for the future?

Does the future in its turn seem to frighten me? I smile at the foolish fancies of my imagination. Is not my future in God's hands?

* * * * *

When all that will happen to me tomorrow, next year, ten years, twenty years in the future, is ordained by him, will I distress myself with the thought that it may not be good for me?

Lord! You be my guide, and choose my lot, as may seem best to you!

2. MEEK UNDER ALL CIRCUMSTANCES

Events are messengers of either divine goodness or justice.

Each has a mission to fulfill, and as it comes from God, why not let it be accomplished in peace?

Painful, heartrending though they may be, they are still the will of God. Watch them as they come, with a little trembling, perhaps even terror, but never let them destroy in the least degree my faith and resignation.

To be meek under these circumstances does not mean awaiting them with a stoic firmness that proceeds from pride or hardening oneself against them to the point of repressing all trembling, no! God allows us sometimes to anticipate, post-pone, or even, when possible, flee them. At any rate, we may try to soothe and soften them a little.

The good Father, when he sends them, sends at the same time the means by which they may be endured and perhaps averted.

Remedies, in sickness.

Love, in trouble.

Devotion, in absences.

Comfort, in weakness.

Tears, in sorrow.

God has created all these, and knowing perhaps that I may fail to find them, he has given commandment to some privileged servants to love, console, soothe, and help me, saying to them, "As you have done it unto one of the least of these my brothers, you have done it unto me."

Oh, welcome then the friendly voice that in the midst of trouble speaks to me of hope. I will receive with gratitude the care that affection presses on me.

With thankfulness I accept the time devoted to me, the deprivation borne for my sake, and I will pray God to bless these kind friends and ask him to say to them words such as these: "All that you have done for mine, I will repay you a hundred-fold."

3. MEEK TOWARD OTHERS

This may seem even more difficult, for it so often appears to us as if others were motivated by malice, but how often it is only the result of temperament, pride, or thoughtlessness. . . . Seeking their own pleasure, without a thought

* * * * *

of the harm they are doing to me. Then why be unhappy about it? I need only to be on my guard.

Never stand in the way of others (when it is not the case of a duty to be fulfilled), and if they sometimes are an obstacle in your way, remove them gently, but do not harm them.

Yielding, submitting, retiring, giving up, this should be our conduct toward the members of our family, and those we call our friends.

The more opportunity you give them for doing what they think right, the more you enter into the feelings they have of their own importance, leaving them a free course of action, so much the more will you be likely to be useful to them and retain your own peace of mind.

It is astonishing how those we never press for conversation open their hearts to us!

Do not try to examine too closely the actions of others or the motives that drive them. If they lack tactfulness, appear not to notice it, or better still, try and think they have made a mistake.

The best remedy for the dislike we feel toward anyone is to endeavor to try and do them a little good every day. The best cure for their dislike to us is to try and speak kindly of them.

Are those around you wicked? Be cautious, but do not lose heart, God will not let them harm you.

* * * * *

How easy for God to hold back the consequences of slander and backstabbing!

God is the shield coming between others, circumstances, and myself.

4. MEEK TOWARD SELF

This does not imply self-complacency, self-indulgence, or self-justification, but simply encouragement, strength, and fortitude.

Encourage yourself in some wearisome monotonous unrecognized work with a thought like this: *God is watching me, and wishes me to do this.* This labor occupies my mind, perfects my soul, and shields me from temptation. . . .

Or in the midst of sadness and isolation, when no one thinks of us, or gives us the smallest token of sympathy, encouragement such as this: "Is not your duty sufficient for me? God requires it of me, and it will lead me to heaven."

Be strengthened to rise again after some failure, some humiliating fault, or some depressing weakness. Rise again lovingly, confidingly, and with the thought, "Never mind, it is a good Father, a kind Master, with whom I have to deal."

Confess your sin, humble yourself, and while awaiting the assurance of pardon, go on with your daily work with the same zeal as before.

* * * * *

Fortitude against the desertion and forgetfulness of others.

We have two things to fortify us: *prayer and labor.*

One to cheer us: *devotion.*

These remedies are always at hand.

B.

Be Humble

1. HUMBLE WITH GOD

Resting always in his presence like a little child, or even a beggar, who, knowing nothing is due to him, still asks, loves, and awaits, feeling sure that hour by hour in proportion to our need, God will provide all that we require, even over and above what is absolutely necessary. Live peacefully under the protection of divine providence. The more you feel your insignificance, weakness, sickness, or misery, the more right you have to the mercy and love of God.

Only *pray* fervently. Let your prayer be thoughtful and reverent, sweet, and full of hope. The poor have nothing left to them but prayer, but that prayer, so humble, so pleading, ascends to God, and is listened to with fatherly love!

Do not have a number of varied prayers, but let the "Lord's Prayer" be ever on your lips and in your heart.

* * * * *

Love to repeat to God the prayer that Christ himself has taught and, for his sake is always accepted.

Look on yourself as a hired servant of God, to whom he has promised a rich reward, at the end of the day he calls *life*. Each morning, hold yourself in readiness to obey all his commands in the way he wills and with the means he appoints.

The command may not always come directly from the Master; it would be too sweet to hear only God's voice. He sends it by means of his ambassadors. These go by the names of *superiors, equals, inferiors,* and sometimes *enemies.*

Each has received the mission (without knowing it) to make you holy. One by subduing your independence, another by crushing your pride, and a third by spurring your unwillingness.

They will, though fulfilling God's command, do it each in their own way, sometimes roughly, sometimes maliciously, sometimes in a way hard to bear. . . . what does it matter, so long as you feel that all you do, all you suffer, is the will of God?

Do your duty as well as you can, as you understand it as it is given to you. Say sometimes to God, "My Master, are you satisfied with me?" and then in spite of boredom, fatigue, aversion, go on with it, faithfully to the end.

Then, whether praise or blame be yours, you will, good and faithful servant, at least have peace.

* * * * *

2. HUMBLE TOWARD OTHERS

Look on yourself as the servant of all, but without pride, or their having any knowledge of it.

Repeat to yourself sometimes the spoken words of the blessed Virgin Mary, "Behold the handmaid of the Lord," and those of our Lord, "I came not to be ministered unto, but to minister," and then act toward others as if you were their slave—warning, aiding, listening, embarrassed at what they do for you, and always seeming pleased at anything they may require you to do for them.

Oh, if you knew the full meaning of these words—all they signify of reward in heaven, of joy and peace on earth—how you would love them!

Oh, if you would only make them the rule of your life and conduct, how happy you would be yourself and how happy you would make others!

Happy in the approval of conscience that whispers, "You have done as Christ would have done."

Happy in the thought of the reward promised to those who give even a cup of cold water in the name of Jesus Christ. Happy in the assurance that God will do for you what you have done for others.

Oh, what matters then ingratitude, forgetfulness, contempt, and scorn? They will hurt, no doubt, but will have no power to sadden or discourage.

Precious counsel, inspired by Christ himself, I bless you for all the good you have done me!

When first those words found entrance to my heart they brought with them *peace* and *strength* to stand against *deception, desertion, discouragement,* and the *resolute will* to live a life more devoted to God, more united to him, more contented, and ever pressing onward towards heaven. Once more, I bless you!

Precious counsels, enlighten, guide, and lead me.

VIII
A Simple Prayer

O Jesus, in the midst of glory, forget not the sadness on earth!

Have mercy on those to whom God has sent the bitter trial of separation from those they love!

Have mercy on that loneliness of heart so full of sadness, so crushing, and sometimes full of terror!

Have mercy on those struggling against the difficulties of life and faint with discouragement!

Have mercy on those whom fortune favors, whom the world intrigues, and who are free from care!

Have mercy on those to whom you have given great tenderness of heart, great sensitivity!

Have mercy on those who cease to love us and never may they know the pain they cause!

Have mercy on those who have gradually withdrawn from holy communion and prayer, and losing peace within, weep, yet dare not return to you!

Have mercy on all we love, make them holy, even through suffering. If ever they estrange themselves from you, take, oh, take all my joys and draw them with the pleasures back again to you!

Have mercy on those who weep, those who pray, and those who know not how to pray!

To all, oh Jesus, grant hope and peace!

IX
Simple Counsels for a Young Girl

Yes, very simple. Listen, my child, and may they sink deep into your heart as the dew sinks in the petals of the flower.

* * * * *

These are my counsels:

Distrust the love that comes too suddenly.

Distrust the pleasure that fascinates so keenly.

Distrust the words that trouble or charm.

Distrust the book that makes you fantasize.

Distrust the thought you cannot confide to your mother.

Treasure these counsels, and sometimes as you read them, ask yourself, *"Why?"* Spirit of God of the child we are addressing, teach her the reason of these sentences that seem to her so exaggerated!

X
A Recipe For Never Annoying Our Friends

This was made by one who had suffered much for many years from numberless little worries occasioned by a relative whose affection, no doubt, was sincere and devoted, but also too ardent and lacking in discretion.

There must be moderation in all things, even in the love we manifest and the care we take to shield them from trouble.

This recipe consists of but four simple rules that are very clear and very precise. Behold them:

* * * * *

1. *Always leave my friend something more to desire of me.*

If he asks me to go and see him three times, I go but twice. He will look forward to my coming a third time, and when I go, receive me the more cordially.

It is so sweet to feel we are needed, and so hard to be thought an intrusion.

2. *Be useful to my friend as far as he permits and no further.*

An overanxious affection becomes tiresome, and a multi-plicity of beautiful sentiments makes them almost unbearable.

Devotion to a friend does not consist in doing everything for him, but simply that which is agreeable and of service to him, letting it be revealed to him only by accident.

We all love freedom and cling tenaciously to our little daydreams. We do not like others to arrange what we have purposely left in disorder. We even resent their overanxiety and care for us.

3. *Be much occupied with my own business, and little, very little, with those of my friend.*

This infallibly leads to a favorable result. To begin with, in occupying myself with my own affairs, I shall the more speedily accomplish them, while my friend is doing the same.

If he appeals to me for help, I will go through fire and water to serve him, but if not, then I do both myself and him the greater service by abstaining. If however, I can serve him

* * * * *

without his knowledge of it and I can see his need, then I must be always ready to do it.

4. *Leave my friend always at liberty to think and act for himself in matters of little importance.* Why compel him to think and act with me? Am I the example of all that is beautiful and right? Is it not absurd to think that because another acts and thinks differently than myself, he must be wrong? No doubt I may not always say, *"You are right,"* but I can at any rate let him *think* it.

* * *

Try this recipe of mine, and I can promise your friendship will be lasting.

XI
Beneath the Eye of God, God Only

As you read these words, are you not conscious of an inward feeling of peace and quietness?

Beneath God's eye, there is something in the thought, like a sheltering rock, a refreshing dew, a gleam of light.

Ah, why always such seeking for someone to see me, to understand, appreciate, praise me?

* * * * *

The human eye I seek is like the scorching ray that destroys all the delicate colors in the most costly material. Every action that is done only to be seen of others loses its freshness in the sight of God. Like the flower, that passing through many hands is at last hardly presentable.

Oh, my soul, be as the desert flower that grows, blooms, and flourishes unseen in obedience to God's will and cares not whether the passing bird perceives it or the wind scatters the petals, scarcely formed.

* * *

On no account neglect the duty you owe to friendship, relatives, and society, but remember each day to reserve some portion of it for yourself and God only.

Remember, always to do some actions that can be known to none but God.

Ah, how sweet to have God as our only witness.

It is the highest degree of holiness.

The most exquisite happiness.

The mother that reserves all that is most costly for her child and the child that prepares in secret some surprise for his mother do not experience a joy more pure or more elevating than the servant of God who lives always in God's presence, whom alone they would please. Or, the loving

* * * * *

heart that enclosing money to some destitute family writes on the cover these words only: "In the name of the good and gracious God."

* * *

The following lines were found on some scraps of paper belonging to some stranger, "They have just told me of a poor destitute woman, I gave them ten dollars for her. It was my duty to set an example. And now, my God, for you, for your sake only, I will send her fifty dollars, which I shall pay from my personal budget.

"Tomorrow, Henry is coming to see me, that poor Henry I loved so dearly, but who has grown cold towards his old friend. He wished to hurt me and does not know that I found it out. Help me, Lord, to remember I have forgiven him, and help me to receive him cordially.

"You alone know all I have suffered."

"What a happy day was yesterday! Happy with regard to heavenly things, for alas, my poor heart suffered.

"Yesterday was a holiday. The snow outside kept every-one at home by their own firesides, and I was left lonely. Ah, yes, my heart felt sad, but my spirit was peaceful. I tried to talk to God just as if I could really see him at my side, and gradually I felt comforted and spent my evening with a sweet

* * * * *

sense of God's presence. What I said, what I wrote, I know not, but the remembrance of yesterday remains to me as some sweet refreshing perfume."

* * *

Perhaps at the last day all that will remain worth recording of a life full of activity and zeal will be those little deeds that were done solely beneath the eye of God.

My God, teach me to live with an abiding sense of your presence, laboring for you, suffering for you, guided by you . . . and you alone!

XII
My Duty toward God

PRAYERS

Slow, recollected, persevering.

Peaceful, calm, resigned.

Simple, humble, trusting.

Always reverent, as loving as possible.

Charitable. Have I not always opportunity to give or to thank?

* * * * *

SUBMISSION

To my calling and to my duty: They come from God, are ordained by God, and lead me to God. To neglect them is to estrange myself from him.

To my pastor, the guide of my soul: He has received the Holy Spirit in order to show me the way. He has God's spirit to guide him.

To my parents: They have God's authority.

To circumstances: They are arranged and sent by God.

LABOR

Begun cheerfully.

Continued with perseverance.

Interrupted and resumed patiently.

Finished perfectly and devoutly.

Repose and care for the body, as in God's sight, under God's protection.

My duty towards my neighbor.

GOOD EXAMPLE

By modest demeanor and simple dress.

By a smiling face and pleasing manner.

Always striving to give pleasure.

Faithfully fulfilling every duty.

GOOD WORDS

Zealous without affectation, encouraging, consoling, peaceful, joyful, loving. These are possible every day.

GOOD DEEDS

Service rendered by material goods, by industry, or by influence.

Ills remedied by excusing, justifying, protecting, defending, concealing faults and mistakes, if possible, by repairing them.

Joys provided, for the mind, by a joyous manner. For the heart, by loving thanks. For the soul, by a word of heaven.

* * *

My Duty toward Myself

COURAGE

In trials and adversity, disturbance, sickness, failure, and humiliations.

Worries that trouble without reason.

Ill temper controlled in order not to pain others.

After failures, to begin again.

In temptations, to withstand them.

ORDER AND METHOD

In my occupation, each at its appointed hour.

In my recreation.

In all material things, for my benefit.

Avoiding errors and constraint as much as conceit and foolishness.

NOURISHMENT

Godly thoughts, read, meditated on and sometimes written.

Books, that elevate and excite love for all that is good and lovely.

Conversations that refresh, rejoice, and cheer, walks that expand the mind, as well as strengthen the body.

XIII
The Power of an Act of Love toward God

Have you ever reflected on this?

Let us consider the exact words that describe it.

"I love you with all my heart, with all my soul, with all my strength, because you are so good, so infinitely good!"

Try and repeat these words slowly so that each may penetrate deep into your heart.

* * * * *

Do you not feel moved as if your whole being, in these words, went forth to God, offering to him life itself?

Do you not feel that in making this act of love, you give far more than if you gave your wealth, influence, or time? No, doesn't this very act seem to bring you riches, strength, opportunities, and all that you possess?

Picture a child standing before you, a child perhaps who may have injured you deeply and yet whose sincerity at this moment you cannot doubt and who is motivated neither by fear nor self-seeking, but simply by a heart seeking forgiveness, and who comes to say to you words of love, such as those above. Do you feel no emotion, no feeling of pity?

I defy you to be without some emotion, not to feel your arms extending, perhaps in spite of yourself, to embrace this poor child, and not to answer: *"I also love you."*

I have yet another test to put to you, poor, alone, guilty, hopeless as you are, seeing only within and around you fears, terror, and damnation.

I defy you to kneel and say these words (laying a greater stress on them because of the resistance you feel), "My God! I love you with all my heart, with all my strength, with all my soul above everything because you are so good. So infinitely good!" and then not to feel that Jesus is moved with compassion, and not to hear his voice, saying to you, "My child, I love you also!"

Oh Jesus, how can we find words in which to express the tenderness awakened in your heart by a word of love from one of your little ones? That heart, so tender, gentle, sensitive, and loving!

A sentence of Faber's may sound unnatural to us, so little spiritually–minded: He says, "God sometimes draws us to him and fills us with love for him, not that he may love us, *that* he always does, but in order to make us *feel* how he loves us!"

An act of love demands but a few moments. The whole of the day, even in the midst of labor, we can multiply it infinitely, and what wonders are brought about by each act!

Jesus himself is glorified, and he pours abundant grace upon the earth.

The Spirit of God, beholding us, listens, draws nearer, and makes us feel we have done right.

The angels above experience a sudden joy and look on us tenderly.

Evil spirits feel their power diminished, and there is a moment of rest from the temptation that surrounds us.

The choir of saints above renew their songs of praise.

Each soul on earth feels the peace divine.

* * * * *

Ah, which of us each day would not renew these acts of love to God!

Ah, all who read these lines, pause for one moment, and from the bottom of your heart exclaim, "My God, I love you! My God, I love you!"

XIV
Be Serious

A statesman retiring from public life occupied himself in his latter days with serious thoughts.

The friends who came to visit him reprimanded him for being melancholy. "No," he replied, "I am only serious. All around me is serious, and I feel the need that heart and mind should be in unison with my surroundings.

"For," he added, with such reverence as to impress all present, "God is *serious* as he watches us. Jesus is *serious* when he intercedes for us. The Holy Spirit is *serious* when he guides us. Satan is *serious* when he tempts us. The wicked in hell are *serious* now, because they neglected to be so when on earth. All is *serious* in this world where we are passing."

Oh, my friends, believe me, it is all true. Let us at least at times be *serious* in our thoughts and in our actions.

XV
Consolation

You distress yourself sometimes, poor thing, because among those who surround you, there are one or two who worry and annoy you. They do not like you, find fault with everything you do, they meet you with a severe countenance and harsh manner, and you think they harm you. You look on them as obstacles to your doing good.

Your life passes away saddened and faded, and gradually you become disheartened. Courage! Instead of provoking yourself, thank God. These very persons are the means of preserving you from humiliating faults, perhaps even greater sins.

It is like the treatment the doctor applies to draw out the inflammation that would kill.

God sees that too much joy and too much happiness, gotten when you receive attention from others, for which you are so eager, would make you careless and lazy in prayer. Too much affection would only deprive you of strength, and you would cling too much to earthly things. So, in order to preserve your heart in all its tenderness and simplicity, he plants there a few thorns, and cuts you off from all the pleasure you believe is yours by right. God knows that too much praise would cause pride and make you less merciful to others. So, instead he sends humiliations. Let them be, then, these persons who unconsciously are doing God's work within you.

If you cannot love them from sympathy, love with an effort of the will, and say to God, "My God, grant that without offending you, they may work my sanctification. I have need of them."

XVI
Personal Worship

The result of worship is, *within,* a fear of sin, *without,* a love for others.

Worship and communion are great aids to sanctification.

Jesus visits the soul, working in it and filling it with his grace, which is shown on all around, as the sun shines forth its light or the fire gives out its heat.

It is impossible but that Christ, thus visiting the soul, should not leave something Christlike within, if only the soul be disposed to receive it. Fire, whose property is to give warmth, cannot produce that effect unless the body be placed near enough to feel the heat.

Does not this simple thought explain the reason that there is often so little result from our frequent worship?

* * * * *

Do you long to receive the grace bestowed by Christ, that shall little by little make you ready for heaven hereafter?

Will you, receiving the God of peace, have for those around you kind words that shall fill them with calmness, patience, and peace?

Will you, receiving thus the God of *love*, gradually increase in tenderness and love that will urge you to sacrifice yourself for others, loving them as Christ would have loved them?

Will you, receiving whom you rightly name the *gracious* God, become yourself gracious? Gracious to sympathize, gracious to forbear, gracious to pardon, and in a small way resemble the God who gave himself for you?

This should be your resolve in your time of worship.

Resolved to obey God's commandments in all their extensiveness, never hesitating in a question of duty, no matter how hard it may be: the duty of forgiving and forgetting some injustice or undeserved rebuke, accepting cheerfully a position contrary to your wishes and inclinations, and application to some labor, distasteful, and seemingly beyond your strength. . . .

If your duty seems almost *impossible* to fulfill, ask yourself, "Is this God's will for me?" and if conscience answers yes, then reply also, "I will do it."

All difficulties vanish after worship.

Generous: depriving yourself of some pleasures that though harmless in themselves, you know only too well, lessen your devotion, excite your feelings, and leave you weaker than before. Generous means doing over and above what duty requires of us.

Conscientious and upright: not seeking to find out if some forbidden thing is really a sin or not, and whether it may not in some way be reconciled to conscience.

Oh, how hurtful are these waverings between God and the world, duty and pleasure, obedience and allurements. Did Jesus Christ hesitate to die for you? And yet *you* hesitate! Coward!

Humble and meek: treading peacefully the road marked out for you by providence, sometimes weeping, often suffering, but free from anxiety, awaiting the loving support that never fails those who trust and renew their strength day by day. Live quietly, loving neither the world, nor its praise, working contentedly in that state of life to which you are called, doing good, regardless of man's knowledge and approval, content that others should be more honored, more esteemed, and having only one ambition: *to love God and be loved by him.*

If this be the goal of your soul, then be sure each special time of worship will be blessed, making you more holy and more like Christ, with more taste and love for the things of God, more sure of glory hereafter.

XVII
After Worship
SELF-SACRIFICE

Lord! Take me and lead me wherever you will! Is it your will, that my life be spent in the midst of such ceaseless toil and tumult that no time is left for those brief moments of leisure, of which I sometimes dream?

Yes! I wish it also!

Is it your will, that lonely and sorrowful, I am left on earth, while those I loved have gone to be near you above?

Yes! I wish it also!

Is it your will, that unknown by all, misunderstood even by those whose affection I prize, I am looked on as useless on account of my stupidity, lack of manners, or bad health?

Yes! I wish it also!

You are Ruler. Oh, my God! Only be yourself the guide and abide with me for ever!

* * * * *

MY MEMORY

My memory! The mysterious book. Reflection of that of eternity in which at each moment is inscribed my thoughts, affections, and desires.

Into your hands, I entrust it, Lord, that you alone may write there and you alone erase!

Leave there, Lord, the remembrance of my sins, but erase forever the pleasures that led to them. Were I to catch but a glimpse of their enticing sweetness, I might again desire them.

Leave there the sweet memories of childhood, when I loved you with such simplicity, and my father, my mother, my family, were my sole affections. Those days, when the slight−est untruthfulness or even the fear of having sinned left me no peace until I had confessed it to my mother. Those days, when I always felt the Spirit of God near me, helping me in my work and soothing my little troubles!

Leave me the remembrance of my first sense of divine forgiveness when, my heart overflowing with secret joy, I cried, "I am forgiven, I am forgiven!"

Leave me the remembrance of your benefits! Each year of my life is crowned with blessings . . . at ten . . . fifteen . . . eighteen . . . twenty years . . . oh! I can well recall all your goodness to me, my God! Yes, receive my memory, blot out all that can estrange me from you, and grant that nothing apart from you may again find a place there!

MY MIND

Oh, by what false lights have I been dazzled! They showed me prayer as wearisome, religious duties too absorbing, social duties as a heavy bondage, devotion, the fate of weak minds and those without affection. Oh, I knew well how false it was, and yet I let myself be almost convinced.

When have I ever been more zealous in labor, than those days when I had fulfilled all my religious duties?

When more loving and devout than on the days of worship?

When have I felt more free, more happy, than when having fulfilled all the duties of my social position?

Lord! Receive my mind, and nourish it with your truth!

Show me that apart from you, pleasures of the senses leave behind only remorse, disgust, weariness, and vanity.

Pleasures of the heart cause anxiety, bitterness, brokenness, and fears.

Pleasures of the mind produce a void, vanity, jealousy, coldness, and humiliations! Teach me that all must pass away . . . that nothing is true, nothing is good, nothing is eternal, but you, you only, O my God!

MY WILL

My deeds are the result of my will, and it is the will only, that makes them of any value.

Oh, then to begin with, I will learn submission! What I wish may not always be good for me. What I am called to do must be right.

Oh Jesus, grant me the grace of obedience, and then let me be called to do many things: works of piety, works of love, self-denial, and brilliant deeds. Deeds that are ignored in my family life or wherever I may be, there are numberless calls for all of these. Lord, behold your servant! May I be always ready when you have need of me!

ALL THAT I HAVE

My God, how richly have you blessed me!

Treasures of love, I offer them to you!

I have relatives, dear ones, You know how I love them . . . Ah, if it be your will to take them from this world before me, though I say it weeping, still I say it. *Your will be done!*

I have friends. . . . If it be your will they should forget me, think ill of me, and leave me alone with that loneliness of heart so bitter and so deeply felt . . . I yield them to you!

I have worldly goods that give me a certain degree of comfort by affording me the means of helping others poorer than myself . . . should it be your will to deprive me of them, little by little, till at last I have only the bare necessaries of life left . . . I yield them to you!

I have limbs that you have given me. If it be your will that paralysis should claim my arms, my eyes no longer see the light, or my tongue be unable to articulate, my God, I yield them to you!

In exchange, grant me your love, your grace and then . . . nothing more, only heaven!

* * *

Oh Jesus, abandoned by all in the garden of Gethsemane, in need then of comfort and strength, you who knows that at this moment there are some on earth who have no strength, no comfort, no support. Oh, send to them some angel who will give them a little joy, a little peace! Oh, if only I might be that messenger! What I must suffer, Lord?

If an outward trouble or inward pain be needful to make of me but for one moment a consoling angel to some poor lonely heart, oh, however sharp the pain, or bitter the trouble, I pray you, grant it to me, Jesus!

O Jesus, you search for lips to tell the love you bear for your children. Lips to tell the poor and lonely they are not despised, the sinful they are not cast away, the timid they are not unprotected. Oh, Jesus, grant that my lips may speak words of strength, love, comfort, and pardon. Let each day seem to me wasted that passes without my having spoken of help and sympathy, without having made someone bless your name, even if only a little child.

O Jesus, so patient toward those who wearied you with their constant requests and ignorance! Jesus, so long–suffering in teaching and awaiting the hour of grace! Jesus, grant that I may be patient to listen and to teach though over and over again I may have to instruct the same thing. Grant me help, that I may always show a smiling face, even though the unkindness of some be deeply felt, and if through physical weakness I show boredom or weariness, grant, O Jesus, that I may speedily make amends with loving words, for the pain I have caused.

O Jesus, who with infinite tact waited, seated at the road–side, for the opportunity of doing good, simply asked a small service of the poor Samaritan woman that you would save and draw to you.

O Jesus, grant that I may feel and understand all the pain that timidity, shyness, or reserve kept buried within the recesses of the soul. Grant me the tact and discretion that draws near to someone without hurting, that asks a question without repulsing, without humiliating, and enable me to bring peace and comfort to the wounded heart.

O Jesus, seeking someone as a faithful giver of your blessings, grant much to me that I may have much to bestow on others. Grant that my hands may dispense your blessings, that they may be as yours when you washed the feet of your apostles, working for all and helping all. Let me never forget that like You I am placed on this earth to minister, not to be ministered unto.

Grant that my lips may speak comforting words and give forth cheering smiles, that I may be as the well by the road-side where the weary traveler stops to drink or as the shade of the tree whose branches laden with fruit are extended over all that pass beneath.

O Jesus, to whom all your children are so dear: whoever they may be, you care for them and remember they are the much-loved children of God! Oh, grant that in all my inter-action with others, I may only see, love, and care for their souls—those souls for whom, O Jesus, you have died. Souls, who, like myself, can call you Father. Souls with whom, near you, I hope to dwell throughout the ages of eternity.